P9-APF-814

James Liu and Stephen Wang
Christians true in China

Edited by Robert Kreider

Faith and Life Press
Newton, Kansas

MENNONITE HISTORICAL SERIES

From the Steppes to the Prairies edited by Cornelius Krahn. 1949.

Plockhoy from Zurik-zee: the Study of a Dutch Reformer in Puritan England and Colonial America by Leland Harder and Marvin Harder. 1952.

Exiled by the Czar: Cornelius Jansen and the Great Mennonite Migration, 1874 by Gustav E. Reimer and G. R. Gaeddert. 1956.

Jakob Huter: Leben, Frömmigkeit, Briefe by Hans Fischer. 1956.

A Century of Witness: the General Conference Mennonite Church edited by Cornelius Krahn and John F. Schmidt. 1959.

Prairie Pioneer: the Christian Krehbiel Story by Christian Krehbiel. 1961.

Mennonite Country Boy: the Early Years of C. Henry Smith by C. Henry Smith. 1962.

A Legacy of Faith: the Heritage of Menno Simons edited by Cornelius J. Dyck. 1962.

Faith in Ferment: a History of the Central District Conference by Samuel Floyd Pannabecker. 1968.

A People of Two Kingdoms: the Political Acculturation of the Kansas Mennonites by James C. Juhnke. 1975.

Open Doors: a History of the General Conference Mennonite Church by Samuel Floyd Pannabecker. 1975.

A People of Mission: a History of General Conference Mennonite Overseas Missions by James C. Juhnke. 1979.

Prairie People: a History of the Western District Conference by David A. Haury. 1981.

James Liu and Stephen Wang: Christians True in China edited by Robert S. Kreider. 1988

Foreword

This fascinating book reveals something of the faith and character of Chinese Christians and some positive aspects of Christian mission work in China.

As a Mennonite missionary working among Chinese people for more than thirty years, I was familiar with the names of James Liu and Stephen Wang through reading reports about Mennonite mission work in China prior to 1949. I, with many others, rejoiced when James Liu's letter reached friends in the United States in 1979 ending the separation and silence of several decades. The lost were found; those feared dead were alive! History came alive through personal correspondence with these men and through a personal visit with James Liu in China.

My unceasing admiration for and appreciation of the Chinese people with their long illustrious history, significant achievements, and fine character traits is reinforced by the stories of these two men. Each exemplifies the ideal Chinese gentleman and scholar figure devoted to family, concerned for harmonious relationships with others, and dedicated to the welfare of country and people. To know them is to know Chinese people at their best.

Christian faith has deeply influenced the lives and careers of these men. That faith enhanced the traditional Confucian virtues and the example of Jesus has shaped their attitudes and actions. Missionaries and mission institutions were significant in instilling and molding their Christian character so they indeed are sons of mission.

Recovery of contacts with James Liu and Stephen Wang helped dispel some of the pessimism and gloom which had shrouded the history of mission work in China, including that of Mennonites. These men give personal evidence that missionaries were a positive influence in their lives. Through their letters, they tell of family members, friends, former colleagues, and former students who have also kept their faith and continue to bear quiet, consistent witness in their daily lives and work. They also share news that worship services are being held, believers baptized, and church buildings reopened in areas where Mennonites worked in northern China. Former mission, educational, and medical institutions, now operated by the government, continue to serve the people. They thus confirm reports from all parts of China that churches not only survived the bitter winter of the Cultural Revolution but are thriving.

Mission circles have often debated and sometimes criticized the policy of sending national Christians overseas for training. James Liu and Stephen Wang are outstanding examples of the successes of that policy. After attending and graduating from Mennonite colleges in the United States, they returned to China to serve in Mennonite and public schools. They paid a high personal price in suffering during the Cultural Revolution for that training, but many students profited from it. Former students, some now holding responsible positions in government and institution, pay tribute to their dedicated teaching.

James Liu and Stephen Wang tell of events beginning in the closing years of imperial China and the century of humiliation through the rise of the new China as one of the world's superpowers. These are stories of the importance and triumph of Christian faith and of enduring friendships between Christians from East and West. The sons and daughters of mission in China also stand as a challenge to us to likewise continue our own heritage as people of mission.

This book is an important contribution to Mennonite mission and church history. Gratitude is due to James Liu and Stephen Wang for sharing their inspiring stories and to all who made the printing of this book possible.

Hugh D. Sprunger

Contents

Foreword   v

Preface   ix

Part One: Humiliation and promise: 1839-1914   1

    1. Father sold the land to feed the family. James Liu   3
    2. Only father was a scholar. Stephen Wang   8

Part Two: The Nationalists come to power: 1915-1933   14

    3. Classmates in six schools on two continents. James
       Liu and Stephen Wang   17

Part Three: The approaching storm: 1931-1937   43

    4. High school principal finds a wife. James Liu   45
    5. A promise to open the mission school. Stephen Wang   49

Part Four: Two wars at once: 1937-1951   56

    6. On the road to Kaifeng, a word from God. James Liu   59
    7. Crossing the Yellow River to flee the war. Stephen
       Wang   63
    8. Five years with Mennonite Central Committee.
       James Liu   72

Part Five: The years after liberation: 1949-1987   80

    9. Jailed in my own school. James Liu   82
  10. Labor, the motherland, and peace. Stephen Wang   94
  11. Letters to friends. James Liu   101

Epilogue   107

Acknowledgments   110

Index   112

Preface

Good fortune lieth within bad;
bad fortune lurketh within good.
  Lao Tzu, sixth century B.C.

Bad things can be turned into good things. . . . China's defeat con-
tained the seeds of victory, while Japan's victory contained the seeds
of defeat. Mao Tse-tung, 1957.

Then what can separate us from the love of Christ? Can affliction or
hardship? Can persecution, hunger, nakedness, peril, or the sword?
. . . in spite of all, overwhelming victory is ours through him who
loved us. Paul, in Romans 8:35-37, New English Bible.

The history of modern China is one of bad fortune and good fortune, defeats and victories, invasions and revolutions, heroism
and treason, warlords and poets. This country of one billion people
is also the story of the quietly victorious in the land: ones like Liu
Zhang-fu and Wang Xinfu, two boys born of peasant families in the
last decade of the great Qing (Manchu) Dynasty. Liu Zhang-fu
came to be known as James Liu; Wang Xinfu as Stephen Wang.
These are their stories

I remember the first Sunday that James and Stephen came to
Bluffton, Ohio. My parents and E. G. and Hazel Kaufman took the
two students, who had just arrived from China, for a picnic on the
banks of the Blanchard River. As a small boy, I listened with rapt
interest as these bright, friendly young men answered a stream of
questions about distant China. For me, it was a window to the
wonderful world of adult talk about churches in faraway places,
friendships with other peoples, and the complexities of a global
community. James Liu and Stephen Wang were the first international students to come to Mennonite colleges in North America
and to return with degrees to serve in their homeland.

In 1951, after the departure from China of the last Mennonite missionaries, P. J. and Frieda Boehr, and the last Mennonite Central Committee worker, Frank Beahn, letters no longer moved back and forth between China and the United States. A wall of silence rose around China. Allies only a few years before, the two countries became enemies during the Korean War. Some news filtered out of China: the establishment of communes, the Great Leap Forward, the rupture of Soviet-Chinese relations, the Great Proletarian Cultural Revolution, the cult of Mao. But no word came from James Liu, Stephen Wang, or the congregations at Kaizhou and Daming.

In 1975 and 1976, in the waning days of the Cultural Revolution, a few of us visited the People's Republic of China on rigidly scheduled tours. We could not visit Kaizhou and environs. In August 1978, with a new climate of openness and moderation under Deng Xiaoping, Grace Liu Yang of Skokie, Illinois, received permission to visit her mother and native home in Kaizhou. While in China, she stopped to see her former teacher, James Liu, and his wife Hazel in Hengyang. Mark Pu-Pok of Evanston, Illinois, a former resident of Daming, relayed James Liu's address to former China missionary Marie Regier Janzen, North Newton, Kansas, and encouraged her to write to her old friend. She wrote, but the letter was returned with the following message: "Refused."

Emboldened by the restoration of China-U.S. diplomatic relations in January 1979, James Liu wrote to his former teacher, Dr. E. G. Kaufman, North Newton, Kansas. Kaufman did not receive the letter, but received a second one mailed on February 20, 1979. In it, Liu wrote: "I am always thinking of you. Will never forget what you have done for me." On January 14, 1979, he wrote to Miss Marie Regier, whom he had known as a missionary and a single woman. He opened with an apology: "First of all, please excuse me for not accepting your letter." Later, when he traveled to the United States and met Marie Regier Janzen in her home, he acknowledged that there might have been danger for him in receiving a letter from a foreigner; however, he explained, he had carefully memorized her address.

In the early months of 1979, Daniel Tsu sent an undated letter from Shanghai to the Mennonite Central Committee at Akron, Pennsylvania. He said: "It is my great pleasure to write to you because of the normalization and reunion of the two great countries." He spoke of being a colleague of Lawrence Burkholder, Dallas Voran, and Frank Beahn in the Mennonite Central Committee's program in Shanghai. He reported that the Hengyang and Kaizhou Mennonites were "all fine."

Following Grace Liu Yang's visit in August 1979 with James and Hazel Liu in Hengyang, the next person to meet James was J. Winfield Fretz, who during 1930-31 had lived with James on the same floor of Lincoln Hall, men's dormitory, at Bluffton College. He wrote to James to report that he planned to lead a tour to China with a stop in Shanghai. When Fretz and his party came to Shanghai, April 12-15, 1980, James and his son Timothy came to meet them. Fretz describes the meeting.

> About nine o'clock in the evening the hotel desk clerk called my room and said, "There is someone here who wants to see you." The management restricted access to the rooms of "foreign friends." I bounded down four flights of stairs and there stood James and Timothy. I took them to my room. I asked James to fill in the events of his life during the half century of silence. James did not answer. He wrote on a piece of paper: "If you have any questions, please write out a list. I will try to answer your questions later." James was telling me that "the walls have ears." I was talking to one who only recently had been imprisoned for three years in his own school. Fear of repetition of such horror was still very real. Later, we went to his uncle's home in another part of the city to talk.

Meanwhile, James and other Mennonites assumed that Stephen Wang, who in 1937 had moved westward with his family, was no longer living. The last word had been that in 1946 he was teaching at a university in Lanzhou, Gansu Province. James received the address of Stephen Wang's brother from Grace Liu, and wrote to him. In response, James received from the brother Stephen's address: Chemistry Department, Northeastern Normal University, Changchun (Zhangchun), Jilin (Manchuria). In June 1980, Stephen visited James and Hazel for two days in their Hengyang home, their first meeting since 1937. Learning of Winfield Fretz's plans to conduct another tour to China, Stephen Wang wrote to him. Stephen, James, Timothy, and Timothy's son John all traveled to Beijing to see Fretz. Their meeting occurred by chance on Sunday, October 11, 1981, in the gardens of the Summer Palace. The following day, the four went with the tour group to the Great Wall and Ming Tombs.

Hearing from Fretz that I was coming to China the following month, Wang wrote to me on October 22 and proposed a meeting in Shenyang (Mukden). Stephen Wang arrived on November 18, 1981, at the Northeast Technical Institute, where Atlee Beechy and I were engaged in discussions regarding the China Educational Exchange program. The university extended V.I.P. hospitality to Professor Wang, friend of their foreign friends.

Out of discussions with Stephen Wang emerged the idea of the writing of his life story. We discussed an outline of chapters, each chapter to be sent as a letter. Stephen was deeply impressed with the vision for the China Educational Exchange program, then being born. He approved instantly the suggestion of writing his autobiography: "It can be my contribution for Chinese-American friendship. It will also be good for my family."

Upon return to the United States, I discussed the idea with Winfield Fretz. We agreed that James and Stephen should be encouraged to write parallel autobiographies. The project began in earnest in 1982 when Stephen came to the United States. The following year, he submitted twenty-six chapters for an autobiography. In 1985, during the visit of James to North America, Edna Kaufman gave him the portable typewriter which had belonged to her husband, E. G. Kaufman. James returned home, began typing his autobiography, and mailed a first draft in 1986.

In 1982, the first North American Mennonites visited Kaizhou. A group related to the Commission on Overseas Mission toured China. Members included Roland and Sophie Brown, Menno and Jessie Brown Gaeddert, Hugh and Janet Sprunger, Peter and Sue Kehler, and Milton and Lavonda Claassen. They met Timothy Liu in Beijing. Dr. Roland Brown and Jessie Brown Gaeddert, who grew up in China as children of missionaries, were permitted a brief visit to their childhood community in Kaizhou. The same summer another group, children of the missionary Pannabecker brothers, visited Kaizhou. In this group were Robert and Alice Ruth Pannabecker Ramseyer, Richard and Wanda Pannabecker, Betty Jean Pannabecker, and Stanley and Anita Pannabecker Bohn. The following year, Elizabeth Beyler, whose father Clayton Beyler had served with the MCC team in China, and her husband, David Kuebrich, visited James Liu. With these visits came renewal of friendship.

James Liu and Stephen Wang's readiness to tell the stories of their lives yields many satisfactions. They share personalized perspectives on critical international events. In bringing to remembrance the story of Christians and the church under test, they nurture all of us in the faith. Their reappearance to describe what has happened to them, their families, former students and congregations—all this is a message of hope. In their telling of a story that extends more than eighty years, the coals of friendship and faith are fanned into flame. We who have shared in this project acknowledge that this has been a pilgrimage with James Liu and Stephen Wang.

Yet, in the background of the stories of James and Stephen

hover shadows of sadness: intimations of careers that might have been; an emerging, vigorous, self-reliant, ably-led Chinese Mennonite church immobilized by invasion, civil war, and prolonged oppression; the beckoning of dreams and visions that could not be fulfilled. The stories of James and Stephen that unfold in these parallel and intertwined autobiographies give witness to an inner fulfillment which persists despite war, imprisonment, humiliation, and shattered plans.

Robert Kreider

A NOTE ON THE SPELLING OF CHINESE WORDS

Since 1958, the pinyin system of writing Chinese ideograms in English letters has gradually replaced the earlier Wade-Giles system. Although James Liu and Stephen Wang have differed in their choice of spellings, we have sought to use the pinyin transliteration, a Chinese-authorized system which is gaining international acceptance. In the case of a few personal names and widely known place names, such as Confucius, Chiang Kai-shek, Mao Tse-tung, Canton, and Tibet, we have kept the more familiar spellings. This includes the older Chinese usage of the hyphen to separate two given names. In parenthesis will usually appear the alternative, normally older, spelling.

Part I. Humiliation and promise: 1839-1914

1839-1842. Foreign trade pressure leads to Opium War; Chinese forced to open five treaty ports.

1858-1860. British-French invasions.

1894-1895. Sino-Japanese War; Japan dominates Korea and Taiwan.

1898. Emperor tries unsuccessfully to reform China in "100 Days"; antiforeign and anti-Christian agitation follows.

1900. Antiforeign Boxer Rebellion suppressed by foreigners. Westerners occupy Beijing.

1901. Henry C. and Nellie Schmidt Bartel, Mennonites, go to China with independent mission.

1904. Birth of James Liu.

1905. China Revolutionary League founded by Sun Yat-sen. Birth of Stephen Wang.

1909. Henry J. and Maria Miller Brown arrive at Bartel mission.

1910. Birth of Margaret Zhang.

1911. Revolution overthrows Qing (Manchu) Dynasty; Sun Yat-sen chosen first president of Republic of China but soon forced out by politicians from the North. Browns begin mission work in Kaizhou; birth of Hazel T. Yang.

1912. Guomindang (Nationalist Party) formed.

1913. Sun Yat-sen fails in second revolution to bring unity.

1914. Outbreak of World War I. General Conference assumes responsibility for Brown mission.

James Liu and Stephen Wang were born in peasant villages in the valley of the great Huang Ho (Yellow) River, which for millennia overflowed often to bring both fertile silt and renewal to the land and loss of possessions and dwellings to the people. Four thousand years ago, in this valley of the Huang Ho, appeared some of the earliest evidences of civilization: towns, commerce, written language, calendars, postal and monetary systems, highways, canals and metallurgy.

In the sixth century B.C., not far to the east on the Shandong peninsula lived the philosopher-teacher-political theorist Confucius, one of the most influential men of all time. The homes into which James and Stephen were born were shaped by traditional Confucian values, codes of behavior and religious creed. The Confucian legacy included belief in the perfectibility of all persons, an emphasis on the ritual norms of order and harmony, and a commitment to the ways of righteousness and filial piety.

The seventy years before the birth of James and Stephen was an era of disaster for the proud and ancient Chinese society. The great powers carved out spheres of influence in a helpless China, established enclaves of Western control in the port cities and along the river valleys. Burdened with feelings of shame and dishonor, young revolutionaries grasped Western republican ideas and overthrew the feeble Qing monarchy. In the cities, people were energized with the exhilarating toxin of change. National unity and recovery, however, eluded the republican revolutionaries. Provincial warlords ravaged the land; the parties of reform wasted their energies in factional fights.

All this was far away from the homes of the Liu and Wang families, where family members tilled the fields, studied for the imperial examinations, and placed offerings at ancestral shrines. Women bound their feet and men wore pigtails. All suffered from the injustices of landlords and merchants.

In the nineteenth century, the first missionaries came to China. They built schools, opened hospitals, and shared the gospel of Christ. Kenneth Scott Latourette in *The Chinese: Their History and Culture*, and John Hersey in his novel *The Call*, described the mission story in China. As many as ten thousand missionaries served at one time in a country of more than four hundred million. Later came the Mennonites—first the Bartels and then Henry J. and Maria Miller Brown (of Mountain Lake, Minnesota, and Freeman, South Dakota). The Browns planted a Mennonite mission in Kaizhou, a city with a population of five hundred thousand, at the southern tip of Hopei (Chihli) Province between Henan and Shandong provinces. That year, three hundred miles to the north in the capital city of Beijing, revolutionaries deposed the last of the Qing emperors, a little boy of six.

1. Father sold the land to feed the family

James Liu

Kaizhou was the headquarters of the General Conference Mennonite Mission in China. Close to the southwest corner of the city wall of Kaizhou (Kai Chow, now called Puyang) of Hebei (Hopei, Chihli) Province, was a village called Hua Yuan Tun. This village had about one thousand homes with twenty family names. The name Hua Yuan Tun means garden. It is said that the people of this village liked to plant flowers.

On June 19, 1904, I was born in this village. China at that time was a feudal society. It was seven years before the Qing (Manchu) Dynasty was overthrown by Dr. Sun Yat-sen, and also seven years before the birth of the Republic of China.

According to Chinese tradition, the third day after the birth, the baby's father visits his father-in-law's family with certain presents. If a female baby is born, the father brings a gift of noodles. If it is a male baby, the gift is two bottles of good wine. When his father-in-law sees the presents, he knows whether the

My father worked for the mission as a gatekeeper: the Liu family in 1933 (James, upper left).

baby is female or male. My father took two bottles of good wine to his father-in-law's family. The whole family was quite happy about it. My father also invited our relatives and friends to a banquet to celebrate my birth.

In our village was a temple in which an idol grandma was seated. Its birthday was February 19. My mother worshiped the idol on its birthday, because she believed that it could bring me good health and a long life. Of course, it was a superstitious practice. According to Chinese custom, people believe that a son can hand down the family name from generation to generation, but that a girl cannot. After her marriage, a girl belongs to another family. A son can inherit his parents' property but a girl cannot.

My mother's name was Wang Jiu-yun. Her parents were farmers. The oldest child, she had two brothers and three sisters. Because her parents were busy with farm work, she had to take care of her brothers and sisters and also did all the housework. Sometimes she helped on the farm, too. My mother was a capable woman. People who knew her all liked her. She was very kind and never scolded me. When I did something wrong, she always talked to me patiently, and what she said was very convincing.

My grandfather made the arrangements for my parents' marriage. The matchmaker was Aunt Liu, my mother's neighbor. After Aunt Liu married, she became my father's neighbor. So she knew the families of both my mother and father. My parents' marriage was harmonious. Whenever they quarreled, my mother always made the concession. She respected my father's mother as her own mother. After my father's death, my mother never said a word about him. When we said something about my father, she only sighed in despair.

My father's parents lived in the countryside. My grandfather, Liu Yu-king, had passed the imperial examination at the county level in the Qing Dynasty so he was called a scholar. He taught at a Confucius type of school for several years and then set up a wine shop in the city of Kaizhou. He was fond of drinking and drank practically every day. Because he drank too much wine, he became mentally ill. Finally, he sold the wine shop and wasted all the money. In 1931, he died at the age of fifty-eight. My grandmother was an illiterate housewife. She died in 1960 at the age of eighty-three.

My father, Liu Lien-hsing, had three younger brothers. The first, Liu Wei-hsing, was a farmer. In 1911, the General Conference Mennonite Mission began its work with Henry J. Brown in the east suburb of Kaizhou. At that time, many people were curious to see the people whom they called foreign devils. Later, the mission held meetings on Sundays. My first younger uncle was not afraid of other people's laughter. He became very interested in the church. He attended catechism class several times and was baptized. Brown asked him to be an evangelist and sent him to a county church at Dongming (Dong-ming), where he was a pastor for many years. My uncle's wife was also baptized. Both of them worked for the Lord until their deaths. My uncle, a faithful Christian, was the most capable man in our family.

My second younger uncle, Liu Wen-hsing, did not like farm work when he was young. Finally he joined the Guomindang (Kuomintang) army. After that the family never heard from him. Later, one of our relatives told my grandmother that he had died during the war among the warlords. My third younger uncle, Liu Tsuan-hsing, still lives in our old village. He is a farmer and has eight children.

Our big family stayed together because of a Confucian teaching that five generations living together makes a good family. People generally believed that the more generations that live together, the more glorious the family is. This paternalistic system played an important role. After my grandfather spent all his money, he wanted to sell the land. At that time our family had eighty mu of land (one mu equals .17 acre). My father and uncles asked my grandfather to divide the land into five parts and finally he agreed. After that, the family was divided into five smaller families. Each family received sixteen mu of land.

When I was a child, people were very superstitious. They believed in all kinds of gods: god of heaven, god of earth, god of wealth, god of kitchen. People worshiped these gods on the first and fifteenth days of each month. During the Chinese New Year, they worshiped the gods three times a day. They also worshiped historical figures, such as Guan Yu, a military strategist, and Zhang Yi, a statesman. The people built temples for them and bowed before their statues.

When a person died, one of his or her children went to a temple to burn incense and paper money before the god, and asked the god to take good care of the dead parent. The children also made a paper house, paper servant, and paper trees of money because they believed that these things are necessary in the other world. Usually, the body of the deceased family member was kept at home for three days before burial. The children invited their relatives and friends to pay respect to the dead and they provided a good meal for the guests.

In 1913, when I was nine, I began attending a Confucian school. I had two teachers, one an officer and the other a scholar of the Qing Dynasty. First, I memorized the Book of Thousand Characters. Then I studied The Four Books, namely the Great Learning, the Doctrine of the Mean, and the Analects of Confucius and Mencius. When I memorized one paragraph, I had to recite it to the teacher and the teacher assigned a new paragraph. If I could not recite it, I was beaten with a ruler. On August 27, the birthday of Confucius, the parents of the pupils entertained the teacher with a banquet and contributed money to buy presents for the teacher. The teacher and pupils paid tribute to Confucius with good food. I studied in this school for three years.

I had a good appetite and ate all kinds of food, hot or cold. I never had stomach trouble and was quite fond of sweets. I fell ill only on rare occasions. My relatives called me "a good eater and sleeper."

My father was fond of traditional opera. When he found out that a local opera was performing around our village, he went to see it. He knew many historical stories so he told me about great heroes such as Zhu Ge-liang, a great strategist, and Lin Ze-hsu, who led the resistance against Great Britain.

My father was strict with me. Once, I bought some candy on credit from Grandpa Liu. When my father found out, he slapped my face. Another time, I led an old blind man across a narrow bridge over a deep ditch. My father heard about it from my second uncle. When I came home my father praised me and gave me a pack of peanuts. Both of my parents hoped that I could be of benefit to other people. They never told me that I should become a great man with a high position in society.

My father, a farmer, worked on his sixteen mu of land. He had some trouble with his eyes so he could not do farm work very well. When I reached the age of eight, I had to help him. At harvesttime, I helped him reap the grain, and in summertime I hoed weeds in the field. When there was no work on the farm, I cut grass. My father had studied in a Confucian school for several years. He could read but could not write. He was good with the abacus. When people sold or bought land, they asked him to calculate for them.

Most of the people in our village were farmers. The land around the village was very fertile. Some people had more than one hundred mu of land and some only had a little piece of land. Some poor people had no land. They rented from the rich and paid a certain percentage of grain to the landlords each year. Sometimes they could not get enough to eat. They raised wheat, corn, millet, sorghum, and beans, but the yield was very low. The farm implements, such as the plow with only one moldboard, were primitive. The rich used cattle to pull the plow, but the poor pulled the plow with their own power. They used a harrow to make the land loose and flat, planted seeds with an old style seed plow, and hoed the field by hand. During harvest, rich people used a cart to haul grain but poor people used wheelbarrows or carried the grain on their backs.

In about 1907, famine came to the Kaizhou area. For several years, too little rain fell to plant seeds. The land was completely dry and some fields cracked. We had no irrigation system and people did not dig wells and canals to channel water to the fields. No one in the area could raise crops.

Nearly every village had a temple in which people worshiped the dragon god, whom they believed was a rainmaker. They performed operas for the rainmaker, but these efforts were useless and the farmers had to find some other way to make a living. During the drought years, not even grass grew, so most people ate bark and tree leaves. Some ate rats and snakes. Finally, they could not find these, so they ate old cotton and cloth. Many died of hunger. In the streets lay people who could not move and who were waiting for death.

My mother's parents had a well, so they irrigated. With a few grains and vegetables, they were able to make a simple living. My mother and I went to my grandparents' home to live. We worked for them and got some food. We led a hard life during the famine. Even though we had something to eat, members of our family became very thin.

During the famine, my father gradually sold all the land to feed the family. Then he went to Kaizhou and finally found a job as laborer for the General Conference Mennonite Mission. At that time, the mission was building a school and a big church, and my father began to attend church and catechism class. A few years later, he was baptized and became a Christian. Then he worked for the mission as a gatekeeper.

My father had a quick temper but was easily moved by other people's words. He sympathized with people in their suffering. After he became a Christian, he often told me Bible stories. He also taught me Christian songs. I still remember the first one he taught, "Jesus Loves Me, This I Know." Once he said to me: "The mission helps you to go on to school. You should study hard and I hope that later you will work for the mission." Because he was good with the abacus, he taught quite a few people to use it. Those people later became renowned for their skills. My father died on January 30, 1942, at the age of sixty-two.

2. Only father was a scholar

Stephen Wang

I was born in a poor peasant family in 1905 in the last phase of the Qing Dynasty. I am the oldest of three sons. My father was a scholar who taught in an old school with only a few students. The school was in a village about three miles away from Wang Tun, our home village. My mother was a typical peasant woman with bound feet. Her childhood home was about three miles from where our family lived. I often called on my maternal grandparents, especially on the Chinese New Year's Day and on other holidays.

My maternal grandfather was a farm laborer who worked for the nearby landlord. He was a good cart driver and his animals were obedient. His family name was Lu, and people often called him Cart Driver Lu. In those days, many of the illiterate peasants didn't have formal names but were named according to their occupations. Everyone had a pet name from childhood which usually followed them into adulthood. We children, however, could not call adults by their pet names.

My mother was a diligent and industrious woman. She was considered illiterate since she had never been to a regular school. But after my father, brothers, and I taught her, she could read the Bible fluently. She really concentrated on her studies. She also studied in Bible classes for women. It seemed strange to me that she knew the words or characters in the Bible, but could not recognize them in other places.

My father had three brothers who all lived together. My uncles were all illiterate peasants; only my father was a scholar. His brothers worked on the farm all day long, and were subjected to endless humiliation, since, in old China, officials and landlords treated peasants high-handedly. My father was intelligent and clever when he was young. An educated man was much admired in those days because he could become a government official, which was an honor for his family and ancestors.

Our family members discussed this and decided to send my father to school so that he could bring honor to our ancestors. Although my father studied in a private Confucian-style school for ten to fifteen years, he didn't have the opportunity to pass the

Most old-style scholars, including my father, could not tell wheat from millet: the Wang family in 1927 (Stephen on the right).

imperial examination. He took the exam twice for other students and they passed, but when he decided to take the exam for himself, it was too late. The imperial examinations stopped suddenly when the Qing Dynasty was overthrown. As a result, he couldn't win honor for the family.

At that time, there was a saying: "If a scholar knows the difference between wheat and millet, he is not a good scholar because he has his thoughts on things other than studying." Most old-style scholars, including my father, could not tell wheat from millet. My uncles were disappointed that my father could not become a government official, and they became unpleasant to him. He did not know how to do farm work, so my mother and I had to do it, even though I was very small. My uncles thought that my mother should do extra work to make up for my father's defects. My mother supported our family by helping out at her mother's house. She often returned with food for us.

In old China, because of the custom that young men and women didn't know each other before marriage, there were many unfortunate matches. I have been told that my mother had a very hard time after she got married. My father couldn't do any farm work, so the family members did not like him. Before our family property was broken up, more than twenty family members lived together, and my mother had to do all the cooking. Her mother-in-law, as well as my uncles and aunts, often tried to annoy her. She had to live in this kind of environment for ten years. Gradually, my mother became stubborn and unyielding. She was an intelligent woman, but developed an impatient disposition.

Our family had two rooms. One was twenty square meters and was used for sleeping, and the other was ten square meters, used as a kitchen. The lodging room was built with bricks and tiles and the kitchen was built with earth and grass. In the kitchen, a bed of grass and earth was connected to the stove. Heat and smoke from the stove flowed through flues beneath the earthen bed. During the winter, we all slept on the warm bed. In the countryside, only the landlord and wealthy people lit fires in the room during the winter. The poor people often slept on heatable earth beds like ours. I slept on the family bed for about ten winters.

When I was small, I was often ill. I couldn't walk when I was three and four years old. One night, my mother discovered that I had diphtheria. She went immediately to the traditional Chinese doctor, who lived in another village some five miles away. People had told her that ghosts—surrounded by brilliant lights—appeared at night around a temple that was on the way to the doctor's village. But my mother still took me in her arms and went to find the doctor.

In the old Chinese society, women were oppressed and despised by the whole family. A woman's only hope was to have a son. As a matter of fact, my mother's greatest hope was that I would be healthy and grow quickly to manhood. Therefore, when she learned that I was ill, she was afraid of neither fatigue nor ghosts. During my serious childhood illnesses, she cared for and cured me with Chinese traditional and herbal drugs.

To this day, I do not know what my mother's full name was. Lu was her surname, but after her marriage a woman was called "the woman of her husband." After having children, she was called "the mother of her child." My father's surname was Wang, so sometimes my mother was called "Wang nee Lu." As a child she had the name "Xiao-mei," which meant "little wintersweet." Like other Chinese women of feudal times, she held the view that man was superior to woman. She never regretted that she had no daughters.

The village of Wang had only ten to fifteen households. Originally it was larger, but many people fled to Shanxi (Shansi) Province during the famine. Wang Tun was one of the five northern-most villages of Henan (Honan) Province. Landlords hired the peasants of our village as laborers. During the famine years, some people became bandits. I remember my grandfather's death. A landlord had demanded that he pay a sum of money for the armed forces of the landlord but Grandfather refused. Bandits came to his house, and he climbed on the roof and fought them but was shot to death.

Our village was located sixty miles east of a mountain called Taihang Shan, between two rivers, Yuhe and Zhanghe. Peasants in our area sowed wheat in autumn and reaped it in the summer. After the wheat harvest, they sowed a second crop and reaped it in late autumn. Because of flooding and other natural disasters, harvests were always poor. Few people had enough to eat.

Two miles from Wang Tun, a country market was held every other day. People from everywhere came to buy or sell goods. On fair days, people pushed and squeezed onto the streets to get closer to the livestock, fish, vegetables, fruits, grains, cloth, and farm implements. I enjoyed the fair and liked to watch the local opera.

In the old days, there were no public schools. The wealthy people opened old-style private schools for their sons, while girls stayed at home to do needlework. My father taught in this kind of school, with Confucian texts that the pupils recited. My father taught me Chinese characters at home. So, even though I didn't have the chance to go to school, I could recognize several hundred Chinese characters.

When I was about ten years old, my father met some Christians associated with the Presbyterian Mission of Anyang (An-yang). Not long afterward, my father became a Christian. He began to teach at Zhangchun (Changchun) school, which belonged to the Canadian Presbyterian Mission of Anyang and was located about eight miles south of Wang Tun.

When my father began believing in Christianity, there was some trouble. Although most people had pigtails, my father cut off his. At that time, all Christian preachers were foreigners whom the Chinese called foreign devils. Chinese Christians, including my father, brothers, and I, were called imitation foreign devils. All of our neighbors and relatives, who believed in Confucianism, opposed my father and fomented discord between my parents. My mother became angry with him because she was afraid he would leave home to go with the foreign missionaries. She took offense at trifles before she, too, became a Christian. At that time, it was the only way for a married woman to struggle against her husband.

Gradually, she changed her mind and obeyed my father. But people of the whole village opposed my father from beginning to end.

In 1914, he began to teach in the boys' primary Presbyterian Mission School at Anyang, the county seat of Henan Province. After one year, my father told me that our family would move to Anyang and that I would go to school there. My brothers and I were happy because Anyang was a city with a railroad. At first, my mother refused to move, but later she changed her mind and went with us. I can still recall an image of my father when we walked along the road between Wang Tun and Anyang. Across his shoulders he carried a long rectangular bag sewn up at both ends, and he sang, "My home is in heaven." I asked my father why he was so happy. He replied, "My son, I've found the real Savior. I'll follow him forever to my death. You'll gradually understand it."

Not long after we moved to Anyang, my father transferred to Jixian to teach at a middle school of the Presbyterian Mission, but our family continued to live in Ping An Zhuang, a neighborhood compound of about ten Christian families. In 1914, I entered first grade at the Presbyterian elementary school for boys, called Binying. School was not difficult for me because my father had already taught me so many Chinese characters. Because of Confucian doctrine that boys and girls be separated, I did not learn to know the girl who would later become my wife, even though she studied in the girls' school at the same time.

I was a day student, but most of the boys in Binying school were boarders. We studied six days a week, and on Sundays, we lined up and marched to church. On Sunday afternoon, students could go shopping or go out to the girls' school, called San Yu. In those days, every Chinese woman suffered binding of the feet, a feudal practice that crippled women physically and spiritually. In childhood, their feet were bound with bandages. In the girls' school, the principal visited the dormitory every evening and punished girls who took off their bandages or socks.

In the high school in Jixian where my father taught, several students came from the Mennonite mission at Kaizhou. These included Wang Wan-chu, Hu Delu, Cheng Guojun, and Liu Guo Xiang. These students asked my father to come to Kaizhou, and in 1917, he finally agreed. So our family moved to Kaizhou, where my father became an evangelist.

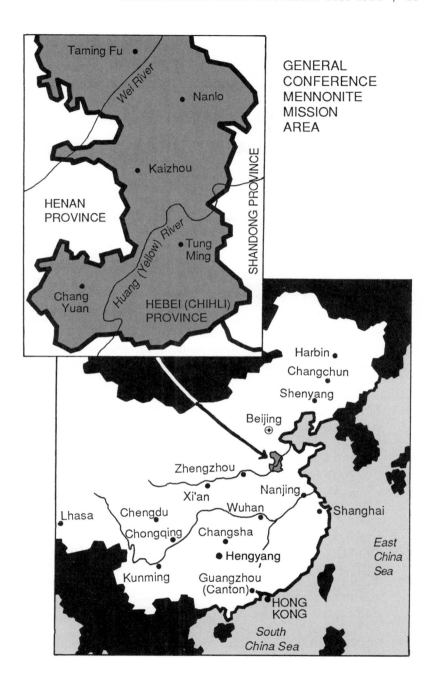

GENERAL
CONFERENCE
MENNONITE
MISSION
AREA

Part II. The Nationalists come to power: 1915-1933

1915. P. J. and Jennie Gottschall Boehr and Talitha Neufeld arrive as missionaries in China.

1915-1918. High tide of Chinese student interest in America; 1,200 Chinese students studying in the United States in 1915.

1916. Warlord period begins. Boys' school built at Kaizhou.

1917. United States enters World War I; October Revolution in Russia. Edmund G. and Hazel Dester Kaufman and Aganetha Fast arrive in China.

1918. Metta Lehman and Christine Habegger arrive. A church building, seating 800, erected in Kaizhou.

1919. Many eyes turn toward the Soviet Union. Japan makes Twenty-One Demands of China. Protests by Chinese against Versailles Treaty. Samuel and Pauline Miller Goering and William and Matilda Kliewer Voth arrive.

1920. General Conference establishes second center at Damingfu with schools, dispensary, and a church seating 1,200.

1921. Chinese Communist party organizes in Shanghai. Dr. Abraham and Marie Wollmann Lohrentz, Elizabeth Goertz and Frieda Sprunger arrive.

1923. S. F. and Sylvia Tschantz Pannabecker arrive.

1924. Russians offer aid to Sun's Nationalist party; Communists allowed to become members; Chiang Kai-shek heads Guomindang's new Whampoa Military Academy.

1925. Sun Yat-sen dies.
1926. C. L. and Lelia Roth Pannabecker and Marie J. Regier arrive.
1926-1928. Chiang Kai-shek launches massive expedition against northern warlords, breaks their power, crushes Communists in "Shanghai massacres," and establishes a new capital in Nanjing. Communists retire and regroup in Kiangsi Province.
1927. "Christian General" Feng occupies Kaizhou area. Missionaries evacuated during civil war; return the following year.
1929. August and Martha Wiens Ewert arrive.
1930. Chiang becomes Christian and marries Mei-ling of powerful westernized Soong family. Chiang launches first of "Bandit Suppression" campaigns against Communists. Elizabeth Goertz founds Yu Jen School of Nursing in Kaizhou.
1933. Great drought in Huang Ho River valley and flood in Yangtze River valley. Japan establishes a puppet government in Manchuria.

When the six-year-old Emperor Xuan Tong, last of the Ching Dynasty, abdicated from the Celestial Throne, two small boys of the emperor's age were growing up in the villages of Hua Yuan and Wang Tun. Soon their parents were drawn by employment and the call of the gospel into an emerging Christian community gathered around Henry and Maria Brown, P. J. and Jennie Boehr, and Talitha Neufeld.

A "period of creative chaos" is James Juhnke's description in *A People of Mission* of these first decades of a new Republican China. Western ideas, technology and values were challenging the old Confucian order. The Chinese were both receptive to new alternatives and hostile to Western dominance. Revolutionary changes came to the Lius and the Wangs who migrated to the ancient walled town of Kaizhou. Some Chinese embraced, and others resisted, change: literacy work among the common people, abolition of child marriages, new rituals for marriage and burial, education for women, Western-style buildings, improved tools and crops, public health clinics and hospitals, publications, Western sports, automobiles, hymn singing, youth organizations, and much more.

Within a sixteen-year period, 1911 to 1927, twenty-three General Conference missionaries arrived. Their field, the six southernmost counties in Chihli (changed to Hopeh or Hobei in 1928, currently Hebei) Province was densely populated with 2,200,000

Feng Yu-hsiang, Kaizhou's warlord, staged mass baptisms for his soldiers in 1927: present with Feng (tall man, center front) were E. G. Kaufman, Talitha Neufeld, and P. J. Boehr.

people in 4,500 villages. In four other county seat towns the mission established schools, clinics, and worship centers. With the arrival of Dr. Lohrentz and nurses Elizabeth Goertz and Frieda Sprunger, a formal medical program began.

In 1913, H. J. Brown baptized the first class of eight Christians in Kaizhou; by 1923, the church had grown to include ten congregations. The young church, led by high school and college graduates, became restive. The Chinese Christians sought a fuller share in church responsibilities, including financial affairs. A special committee was appointed to resolve issues of authority. After twelve years of negotiation, the mission and church accepted a new constitution.

In 1927, a "Christian general," Feng Yu-hsiang, was the warlord controlling the Kaizhou area. He staged mass baptisms for his soldiers. In the same year, General Chiang Kai-shek, who in three years would become a Christian, swept through the area on his Northern Expedition. Many hoped that, with Christians in high offices, a new national openness to the Christian faith was dawning. During this year of civil war, at the urging of the American consulate, missionaries fled the field. When they returned in 1928, the Nationalists were firmly in power in the new capital of Nanjing (Nanking).

In James and Stephen's accounts, we see the larger national developments that touched them: the political and educational mission of the Northern Expeditionary Force, the exhilarating pull of higher educational opportunities in America, the national idealism of young college graduates returning to their homeland.

3. Classmates in six schools on two continents

Stephen Wang

Henry J. and Maria Brown had founded the Mennonite Mission in Kaizhou in 1911, and my father, one of its earliest preachers, worked well with the missionaries. He was an eloquent speaker, fluent and clever. He could explain the profundity of the gospel in simple terms, so common people liked to listen to him. On the other hand, he often quoted the classics and included old sayings in his speeches, so scholars liked to hear him, too. Many people were moved to become Christians after they heard him preach.

My father was a pious adherent of Christianity. He often told me that he was saved by the Lord. Before he became a Christian, he idled away his time playing cards and smoking opium with his friends. After he became a Christian, he stopped seeking pleasure with that pack of rogues; he became a new man. Thank the Lord, he was saved. He often told his own story to those whom he met, to persuade them to follow Jesus Christ.

James Liu

The General Conference Mennonite Mission began when I was seven. Two years later, I attended church and Sunday school with

Many people were moved to become Christians after they heard my father preach: the elder Wang (far right) with missionaries Boehr and Voth and other evangelists in 1927.

my father. In 1916, the mission opened an elementary school. Some of my cousins who attended enjoyed the school. I asked my father to send me, and finally he agreed. I was very happy. My father paid eight dollars for my board the first year, but the following year he could not afford to send me. The principal, Rev. Brown, found out that I was not in school and sent for me. He told me that the mission would pay for my school expenses, and from that time on, it did.

Stephen Wang

Kaizhou was a county seat of Hebei (Hopeh, Chihli) Province and had a population of two to three hundred thousand. Like other cities in old China, it was surrounded by city walls that offered protection from armed rebellions. Kaizhou was on the north side of the Yellow River, which flooded often. Several times in my memory, water came over the dike on the south side of the city, and the missionaries offered flood relief. The Mennonite mission station was located in the east suburb of Kaizhou. At that time, the city had no other Christian churches except for a Catholic church.

Ghosts seen in the school yard at Hua Mei

The name Hua Mei meant "Chinese American." Hua Mei School was divided into boys' and girls' schools. I entered the third grade of the boys' school, which had about fifty students. Nearly all the pupils were children of Christian families, and the teachers, who were also Chinese Christians, lived with the students in dormitories, where groups of ten to twelve students slept in rooms with plank beds. Sometimes the students played jokes on the teachers by placing obstacles in their way. Teachers who became angry sometimes knocked the heads of the students. For awhile, the school was troubled by students who claimed to have seen ghosts in the school yard. Mr. Hu, a teacher, also provoked turmoil when he ran from his bed without clothing and was later discovered to be mentally ill.

During our elementary school years, I did not know how to study; I mainly liked to play. Classmate James Liu, who was a year older, was a better student. He was clever and diligent. He was always at the top of our class, and I was usually in third place. James was trustworthy and had the ability to settle disputes among our classmates. I had great respect for James—he was like an elder brother.

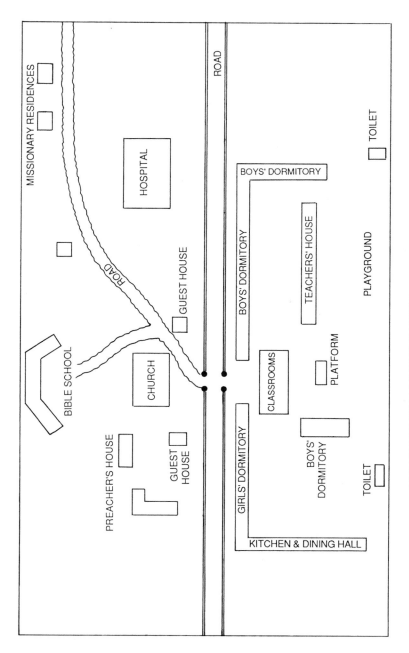

JAMES LIU'S SKETCH OF THE KAIZHOU MENNONITE MISSION COMPOUND

James Liu

One of my intimate classmates was Stephen Wang. We went to school together for sixteen years, from primary school through college. Stephen was well liked. He could play all kinds of ball games and excelled at track. A high tenor, Stephen was also a good choir leader. When we grew older and left Hua Mei School to continue our studies, we always asked to live together.

During our years at the mission elementary school, all the pupils had to go to Sunday school and church services. The school held a morning worship service every day except Sunday. In the beginning, we had two Confucian teachers, Wang Hsien-Deng and Liu Yue-king. Both of them became Christians. Later we had teachers who had graduated from mission high schools. In the lower grades, we learned Chinese language, math, cultivation of moral character, music, and gymnastics. In the higher grades, we also studied geography, history, and natural science. Besides these, we had Bible courses.

Missionaries: honor in a pockmarked face

In the fifth grade, I began to study English. Hazel Kaufman was our English teacher. She gave me the English name James. I also attended catechism class. Some of my relatives said to me, "If you

Kaufman was farsighted and had lofty ideals: traveling by wheelbarrow in 1920 with mission board president J. W. Kliewer (left).

believe in Jesus and are a Christian, the missionaries will take
you to another country and dig out your heart and eyes." As a
result, I was scared and stopped attending catechism class. Later, I
realized that their statements were not true, and resumed attendance. I was baptized in 1920 at the age of sixteen.

Stephen Wang

I learned to know a number of missionaries at Kaizhou. Henry J.
Brown, founder of the General Conference Mennonite Church in
China, was worthy of the title of pioneer missionary. Rev. Brown
had a serious and stern character, and occasionally he went to
local government offices to intervene for people involved in disputes. Foreign missionaries had some influence on certain matters, and the Chinese government officials dared not refuse their
requests.

James Liu

Rev. Brown, our primary school principal, was an impetuous person; it was difficult to change his mind. But he was a hard worker.
Mrs. Brown was a patient, kindhearted woman.

Stephen Wang

E. G. and Hazel Kaufman pioneered the educational work of the
Mennonite mission. Rev. Kaufman was farsighted and had lofty
ideals; under his leadership, the school prospered. He had a deep
love for youngsters, and James and I benefited from his precise
teaching of English. He taught us how to play American football
and baseball. He also led the students in a chorus, and we performed on holidays. E. G. Kaufman had the misfortune to contract
smallpox and nearly lost his life. Ultimately, he got a pockmarked
face. For him, that face was the greatest honor, for it showed that
he had made contributions to the Chinese people, and we could
never forget him.

James Liu

I admired Rev. Kaufman's resourcefulness and courage. He was
one of my best teachers and friends. He influenced me greatly.
Mrs. Kaufman was a good teacher and helper of Rev. Kaufman. In
1922, Rev. Kaufman sent me to Zi Bien high school in Kaifeng
(K'ai-feng). The day before I left, my mother called my fiancee to
come to our home. We talked together for some time. My aunt
reported this to Rev. Brown and he asked Rev. Kaufman to call me
back right away from Kaifeng. When I came back to Kaizhou, Rev.

Kaufman said that according to Chinese custom, an engaged couple should not see or talk to each other. We had broken the custom. I admitted my fault and promised never to do it again. Then Rev. Kaufman sent me back to Kaifeng, where I had missed my schoolwork for two weeks.

James Liu

The first car I saw belonged to Rev. Kaufman. One day he drove to our home to visit us. Almost all the people of the village came out to see the car. Some of them thought there must be a demon in it making it go. In 1923, Hazel Kaufman bought a new piano and taught me to play. I was happy, for that was something I had never dreamed of. Rev. Kaufman told us of the ways of American people, such as freedom to choose one's marriage partner. That made us laugh.

Stephen Wang

Aganetha Fast was a conscientious woman who sometimes went to the countryside to preach the gospel. One can imagine that it must have been difficult for a single woman to travel in the rural areas. She was strict with herself but broad-minded with others, and left a deep impression on the people who knew her.

James Liu

Marie J. Regier was a good English teacher. She knew how to lead the students in Christian life, and she was well liked. Samuel and Pauline Goering were kindhearted and charitable people. Dr. Abraham M. Lohrentz was a good doctor. He examined a patient carefully and made detailed inquiries. Marie Lohrentz was a good teacher and was strict with students. Rev. Floyd Pannabecker was a gentleman who spoke Chinese elegantly and more fluently than other missionaries. Sylvia Pannabecker was good at working with young people.

Stephen Wang

Floyd Pannabecker was fond of music and bought a Chinese reed instrument made somewhat like a small pipe organ. We called it "pipe organ holding in both hands." He learned to play it well. Another musician was Rev. Peter Boehr; people enjoyed listening to him sing. Rev. Boehr was our primary school principal for one year. He was zealous in the Lord's work.

I learned to know William C. and Matilda Voth. His work was mainly to build housing for the missionaries, and I discovered that he was a capable and versatile person. The style of the buildings was unusual; people called the buildings foreign. These early foreign lodgings in Kaizhou were built with the labor of Chinese bricklayers, tilers, plasterers, and carpenters. I knew from these workers that William Voth treated them graciously, but that he also had a conscientious and meticulous attitude toward the work.

Jennie Boehr was tenderhearted and well liked. Metta Lehman brought up two orphans whom she had found wandering in the streets. One of them, Li Guang-ming, later became an evangelist and worked in a Mennonite church in Shanxi (Shansi) Province. Elizabeth Goertz did a remarkable job with patients, and also took in and brought up several orphans. Frieda Sprunger supported my younger brother in his studies at a Bible school in Tengxian, Shandong (Shantung) Province, and later in his medical studies.

James Liu

Dr. Lloyd Pannabecker was a good doctor. In the summer of 1933, a mosquito bite on my right foot became infected. The flesh became black and it was serious. Dr. Pannabecker cut the black part off. Then the new flesh grew back but no new skin grew. Dr. Pannabecker grafted some skin onto the foot. I stayed in the hospital for four months. Dr. Pannabecker, with God's help, saved my life.

Stephen Wang

Over a period of several years, my mother came to believe in Jesus Christ. In 1918, she asked my father to help her become baptized. Rev. Brown officiated at the service in the Mennonite church at Kaizhou. Once or twice a year, a certain number of people were ready to be baptized into the Christian faith. They went to the platform and knelt, and Rev. Brown put both his hands on the head of a baptismal candidate and prayed. Then he sprinkled some water on the person's head and prayed again. After all were baptized, they got up and went back to their seats.

My mother was an eloquent speaker. Around 1920, before she became an evangelist with my father, she worked closely with Matilda Voth at Kaizhou. In response to famine, the mission asked my mother to organize a group of women to spin cotton thread and weave cloth. The mission paid everyone a certain amount of corn, and my mother drew her share. Each evening we ground the corn into flour using millstones.

High School: Christian teachers inspired us

During the 1930s, some of the missionaries were discouraged that many of the young people who went through the Kaizhou mission schools later left the church. Many of these students, who attended for several years, came from non-Christian homes. The missionaries could not hope that all who left the school would remain Christian—that is impossible. As time passed, some Chinese students, who worked in the countryside where there was no church, forgot their beliefs. But students who came from Christian families or whose environment supported their beliefs remained good Christians. There are many examples of this.

Hua Mei Junior High School, one of the few institutions of higher education in the district, served as an alternative even for non-Christians.

Stephen Wang

I spent my high school years in three places: 1922-23 at Zi Bien High School in Kaifeng in Henan (Honan) Province; 1923-24 at Hua Mei Junior High in Kaizhou; 1925-28 at Porter Senior High, Dezhou, Shandong Province.

After we graduated from the mission elementary school in 1922, James and I and several other students went to study at Zi Bien High School, a Baptist school in the south suburb of Kaifeng, 120 miles south of Kaizhou. It was the first time any of us had traveled so far from home. James was elected leader of the group, responsible for taking care of all the arrangements during our five-day trip. When we arrived, we were interested in all the sights of what was at that time the capital of Henan Province. Kaifeng, a historic, flourishing city, contained many civic and cultural institutions.

James and I stayed in a second-story dorm room and slept on spring beds without mattresses—we were happy if not very comfortable! The school was under a four-year system and had 120 students. The principal, an American Baptist missionary, was a serious man whom we nicknamed "Big Nose Shi." Most of our teachers were graduates of Hujiang University in Shanghai, a Baptist institution. I began to study English. The American teachers spoke English to us, and we also had a Chinese teacher of English grammar.

James Liu

In the spring of 1923, the students staged a strike because of compulsory religious activities. Some students tore up their Bibles and left the school. The Christian students did not want to leave, so the non-Christian students called them foreign slaves and threatened them. The Christian students had to leave for the time being. Finally, the provincial government officers settled the problem. In 1924, the anti-Christian movement swept through the entire country. Most of the missionaries learned a lesson from this movement and changed their methods of preaching.

That summer, the educational system of China changed from a four-year to a six-year system (three in junior high and three in senior high). A new school, named Hua Mei Junior High School, began in our mission at Kaizhou. Rev. Kaufman was the principal. We returned to the mission school to enter the first graduating class and to study English under Marie Lohrentz.

Stephen Wang

This was a great event in the Mennonite mission field, since many students of the elementary school could continue their education without going away. Hua Mei Junior High School, one of the few institutions of higher education in the district, served as an alternative even for non-Christians. People of the area, whether or not they were Christian, were interested in the school. Some of our teachers were graduates of Qilu University, a Christian school in Shandong Province. By opening the new junior high, E. G. Kaufman rendered a great service.

James Liu

I graduated in 1924 and then taught at the attached primary school for one year, which was quite an experience! Besides my regular work, I taught Floyd Pannabecker the Chinese language.

In 1924, the Chinese people waged the First Revolutionary Civil War under the leadership of the Chinese Communist party against the imperialists and the northern warlords. The Chinese people suffered a great deal because of the fighting among the warlords. The struggle against warlords swept the whole country. Our mission at Kaizhou became occupied by a warlord named Liu He Zi. When he had to leave, his soldiers robbed us of goods and money. His presence interfered with the mission work, and most of the missionaries and their families moved to Tienjin (Tientsin) and other coastal cities.

Stephen Wang

In 1924, the mission board asked my father to begin a church at Zingfeng, a town fifteen miles north of Kaizhou. I spent a year teaching at a church grade school there. My father was overjoyed, because I was the eldest son and could begin to earn money for the family. Earlier, during my primary school years, my father had told my mother that I couldn't accomplish anything. It was at Zingfeng that my father began to have a good impression of me. If he were still alive, he would perhaps be satisfied with my work as an adult.

After the summer of 1925, James and I and several others continued our education in Dezhou, Shandong Province, at Porter Senior High School. Dezhou was two hundred miles away, and we traveled there by foot and by riverboat. James was again in charge of our group throughout the journey.

James Liu

At Porter, I took liberal arts courses. There was an organization called Christian Fellowship, which brought students together to study the Bible and to believe in Jesus Christ. I joined this group and was in charge of it for one year. We had prayer meetings, and on Sundays, went out to the countryside to preach the gospel to the villagers. Our Bible teacher, Rev. Wang Jing-wen, was our adviser. There was also a YMCA in the school which most students joined. I was elected chairman of the organization for two years. I enjoyed school life very much. In 1927, I heard that Charles Lindbergh was the first person to fly across the Atlantic Ocean. I saw an airplane for the first time in Dezhou in 1927.

Stephen Wang

Dezhou was the center of China's great plain. But drought plagued the area, and the people of the Dezhou region were poor. Porter was sponsored by an Anglican mission, and many of its graduates went on to Qilu University in Shandong Province and Yenjing University in Beijing (Peking). Porter's American principal, Mr. Matthews, wrote with his left hand, which I considered a wonder since I had never seen such a thing.

At Dezhou, I changed my name. When I went to register and told Mr. Matthews my name, Wang Huan-zhang, he smiled and said, "We don't want another Wang Huan-zhang, we have another student here already by that name." As a result, I changed my name to one which was similar, Wang Xin-fu.

At Porter, we had several teachers who not only excelled in the classroom but who also inspired us by their daily life. These teachers were Christians. We often went to the room of Mr. Chapman, our geography and English teacher, to chat. He talked humorously about America and we enjoyed him very much. I learned much spoken English from him.

James Liu

After Mr. Chapman left for Greece, he taught in an American college in Salonika. He arranged for a Greek student to write to me, and my English improved through our correspondence.

Stephen Wang

We also had some non-Christian teachers who were not as good. I began to think that a person must become a Christian before becoming a good person. I believed that a Christian loved all human beings and was devoted to his work because that is what our heavenly Father desired. Although I had been baptized in junior high school, I had understood little of its significance then. As I grew, I gradually understood that a person must acknowledge guilt before God and then ask for God's forgiveness, in order to become a true Christian.

Father shot by bandits

On November 28, 1927, my father, who was in his fifties, died after being shot by bandits. My parents had been living in a hut near a landlord's manor during an evangelistic drive. The bandits thought erroneously that my parents were relatives of the landlord, so they fired on them. The news of my father's death came to me about two weeks later, after he had been buried. My brothers were at Kaizhou, but I knew nothing of the funeral arrangements until afterwards. Chinese custom requires that a man must be buried on his own land if possible. After temporary burial in the mission cemetery, one of my brothers took the body of my father to his old home near Anyang.

In 1982, many years after my father's death, I received a letter from my friend, the missionary doctor Lloyd Pannabecker. On October 20, 1927, he had opened the Mennonite mission hospital at Kaizhou. He had attended my father in his last days. The following is taken from his diary:

> *November 2.* Our first inpatients, a Mr. and Mrs. Wang . . . arrived at noon. Both had gunshot wounds through the right leg near the knee. He has a compound fracture of the tibia.
> *November 10.* Mrs. Wang is getting along well. Mr. Wang doesn't have much pep, his temperature has been up (104 degrees). We have cleaned out his wound and irrigated it thoroughly. He does not seem to have much resistance.
> *November 27.* I have given up hope that he will be able to overcome his infection. He must either have an amputation or we give up hope of saving his life.
> *November 28.* The operation was completed but the patient died.
> *December 2.* The death of Mr. Wang struck his family pretty hard. Mrs. Wang . . . wept bitterly for a time. It is, in China especially, a most serious situation when the head of the family dies. . . . The future must look bleak. However, being a Christian, I am sure her faith was a great help.

In the summer of 1928, James and I graduated from Porter Senior High School. At that time, the First Revolutionary Civil War was being waged by the Chinese people under the Chinese Communist party, against the imperialists and northern warlords. In the summer of 1928, a propaganda team of the Northern Expeditionary Army reached Dezhou. We didn't know much about the revolution or the Northern Expedition, but we needed money, and James persuaded me that we should join the propaganda team.

Yenjing University: horizons broadened

Our task was to spread word among the masses so that they would understand the significance of the Northern Expeditionary Army. We told people about the suffering caused by the wars among the warlords. Since the Northern Expedition was drawing to a close, we did little work, but we traveled three hundred miles by foot from Dezhou to Xuzhou. It was exhausting, and I regretted joining the propaganda team. At Xuzhou, we took the train to Nanjing (Nan-ching), and officials there invited James and me to continue working with the team. We told them that we wanted to continue

Our high school examination results qualified us to enter Yenjing University without taking entrance examinations: Stephen and James, 1929.

our studies so that we could make a greater contribution to the country. The officials, happy to hear this, paid our wages and gave us an additional hundred dollars.

James Liu

When we got back to the school at Dezhou, we discovered that E. G. Kaufman had sent us a letter from America. When we opened it, we found a check for us to go on to college. We immediately asked our principal to write to Yenjing University. In September 1928, we went to Beijing to enter the university.

Stephen Wang

Yenjing University was one of the best church universities in China before the revolution. Our high school examination results had qualified us to enter the university without taking entrance examinations. We were "test students" until we passed the mid-term exams and became regular students. Located between Beijing city and the Summer Palace, the school buildings were beautiful, with carved beams and painted rafters. Their exteriors imitated the old Chinese palatial architecture. Inside, however, the decor was Western in style.

James Liu

Yenjing University was located at the west suburb of Beijing, the capital of China as well as the headquarters of the Qing and Ming dynasties. The university was run cooperatively by several denominations. I took part in the university church choir and sang each Sunday. On Christmas Eve, 1929, we sang Handel's *Messiah* in the university auditorium. At the beginning of my sophomore year, I decided to major in sociology and minor in education, and I also took courses in economics, history, geography, English, Chinese, and German.

Stephen Wang

Our only free time was on Sundays, and those we always spent in church. We worked hard at Yenjing University, studying and trying to earn money. We rarely took in entertainment or paid attention to political affairs. We had no money to attend the films shown on weekends at the university, so we studied in the library during the showings.

Student movements that were popular elsewhere in China, such as the anti-Christian movement, could not take place on the campus. Yenjing was sponsored by Christians, and students were serious about getting a diploma from this famous school. I was involved in a group of nine young men who had graduated from missionary high schools. We all had financial difficulties so we commiserated with each other and established a strong fellowship. We encouraged each other to be upright and devout Christians and to maintain our group fellowship.

James and I paid for all our expenses except for board. We often consulted each other on how to tide over our financial difficulties. At first, we thought we would be able to stay only briefly, but we kept seeking typing jobs and other work opportunities. During the summer of 1929, there was a great drought in Rehe Province, now the Inner Mongolia Autonomous Region, and the Chinese Foreign Relief Unit wanted to draw water from the Yellow River into the irrigation canal. The engineers for this irrigation project were American missionaries, and the organization recruited translators. Although many people feared pestilence due to the drought, James and I were eager to earn money for the next school year. We signed up for two months and during our summer vacation, we each earned 120 dollars. During our time there, many people died of hunger.

Most of the Yenjing students were the children of capitalists or government officials. There were also many overseas students who

When we grew older and left Hua Mei School to continue our studies, we always asked to live together: graduating class in 1924 (James in back row, fourth from left; Stephen, seventh) with their teachers E. G. and Hazel Kaufman and Marie Lohrentz.

came from Indonesia and the Malay Peninsula and Archipelago. They were all rich, and some wore Western-style clothes and leather shoes and drove cars. Some idled away their time in pleasure seeking and didn't pass the midterm examinations, so they had to leave.

James Liu

Because many of the students were rich, some people called Yenjing University "the school for royalty."

Stephen Wang

During our second year, James and I didn't have enough money, so we lived in the attic of the dormitory. It was cold in winter and hot in summer, but we had to pay only nine dollars a semester for our room. During the winter I wore only thin clothes. Every time I went to class from one building to another, I ran.

James Liu

During the second year, Stephen and I each bought a pair of leather shoes, which we wore during the daytime. At night, we changed into our cloth shoes to save the shoe leather.

Stephen Wang

Many of us who really struggled at Yenjing University later had the opportunity to go abroad. A Chinese proverb says: "Poverty gives rise to a desire for change."

Awareness of the outside world

Dr. Leighton Stuart was president of the university. He could speak Chinese well and often visited with staff and students. His parents had been missionaries in Zhejiang (Chekiang) Province, where he was born. He frequently traveled to America to solicit funds for the school. Unfortunately, he became the American ambassador to China shortly before liberation, and in that position, helped the decadent Guomindang fight against the Chinese Communist party and Liberation Army. As a result, Dr. Stuart was dishonored in the eyes of the Chinese people.

James Liu

Today many Yenjing University graduates work in the central government. Yenjing University made many contributions to the people of China. I am proud to have Yenjing University as my alma mater.

Stephen Wang

When I arrived in Beijing in 1928, I thought that a person who lived in the city was fortunate, yet at the same time I thought that the emperors of the dynasties were too luxurious. They sought ease and comfort at the expense of the suffering poor. During my two years at the university, I surely broadened my horizons. I am happy to have had the opportunity to attend Yenjing University.

James Liu

While I was in school I tried to concentrate on my studies, so I paid little attention to political affairs. But I respected several political leaders, especially Dr. Sun Yat-sen, who in 1911 founded the People's Republic of China. Although he faced difficulty in leading the revolution, he was concerned with helping the Chinese people. I also respected General Feng Yu-hsiang, whom the Chinese Christians called "the Christian general." He invited pastors to preach the gospel to his soldiers, and many of the soldiers were baptized.

Stephen Wang

By 1930, I was twenty-seven and had traveled to many places in China, but I knew little of the outside world because I had studied in church schools. Politically, I was nearly ignorant, even though during my school years, China was always in a turbulent and unpeaceful situation. The church school in old China was somewhat of an island, showing no concern for the country or society.

I do not recall discussions of world or political affairs with any of the missionaries, because I was ignorant of these matters, and also because there was no opportunity to talk about them in the circle of the church. Most missionaries didn't want young men to talk about or join political movements.

E. G. Kaufman was the only missionary who stood for running schools in the mission field. There was, of course, a primary school in our mission field at Kaizhou before he came, but the missionaries at that time did not want to let young people receive further education. It was E. G. Kaufman who sent us to Kaifeng to continue our studies and who later proposed that we go to Dezhou to study at Porter Senior High School. In 1925, he and his family left China. When he learned that we were studying at Yenjing University, he responded with great interest and happiness. He then planned for us to continue our studies in America, to foster our affection with the Mennonite church and the American people. I am steadfastly thankful to E. G. Kaufman for his encouragement, and I will remember him forever.

Other missionaries who helped us included Samuel J. Goering and Abraham M. Lohrentz. Rev. Goering was the only missionary who stretched out his hand to help us through our financial difficulties at Yenjing University. Dr. Lohrentz, together with Dr. Kaufman, made the arrangements for James and me to go to America in 1930. More than fifty years later, when I had the opportunity to go to America again, my first thought was to look for the children of Dr. Kaufman and Dr. Lohrentz to express my gratitude. Fortunately, I saw them all.

The trip to America

From the history of China, one learns that the Chinese were strongly spirited people. They never went down on their knees in surrender or knuckled under oppression. As I grew older, I studied the history and geography of China, which broadened my knowledge and enriched my patriotic feelings. During my years at Yenjing University, I developed a will to make the country strong. Although the Chinese experienced much suffering from both pov-

E. G. Kaufman planned for us to continue our studies in America, to foster our affection with the Mennonite church and the American people: farewell group with James and Stephen (center right).

erty and impoverishment, I never became utterly disheartened, because I knew that poverty gave rise to a desire for change.

James Liu

In the spring of 1930, Dr. E. G. Kaufman wrote Stephen and me a letter from Bluffton College. He said that our English was good enough for us to go to the United States to study. How wonderful the news was! Before long, Dr. Mosiman, president of Bluffton College in Ohio, sent the certificates admitting us to Bluffton. We showed the papers to the university officers and asked them to assist us in obtaining a study leave and our passports. Soon the school office had those papers.

Stephen Wang

We were overjoyed to learn that we could go to the United States through our personal relationship with E. G. Kaufman. We went to Tienjin (Tientsin) to finalize the arrangements.

James Liu

We sailed from Tienjin at the end of July. The ship followed the

We sailed from Tinjin at the end of July 1930: James and Stephen with medical student Hu Hsin Yu (center).

coast of Korea and got to Kobe, Japan, three days later. We stayed in Kobe for a few days before transferring to another Japanese ship, which was on its first voyage to America. From Kobe, our ship sailed to Yokohama, passing Mt. Fuji. For two days we visited Yokohama and Tokyo, Japan's capital city. Our stay in Japan was a tremendous experience for us. After two weeks at sea, our ship reached Vancouver Island, Canada, and the next day we arrived at Seattle.

When we landed, Joseph Habegger, a friend of E. G. Kaufman, met us at the pier. The next morning, he took us sightseeing and then to the railway station where we started for Chicago. In Chicago, Dr. Kaufman stood waiting for us as we got off the train. We had not been expecting him to meet us, and at first we did not recognize him. Then we cried out, "Dr. Kaufman!" We began to shake hands and talk. It was wonderful to meet him again.

Stephen Wang

He took us to a Chinese restaurant in Chicago, where we ate chop suey. This was something from South China, but we did not know of it at all. Americans considered it typical Chinese food.

James Liu

At the restaurant, we liked the Chinese noodles. But the bowl was so big that when we saw it we thought, "Oh, how can we eat all of this!" And Dr. Kaufman said, "Eat as much as you can. If you cannot finish it, that's all right." Then he showed us around Chinatown and the University of Chicago.

That afternoon, we started for Bluffton. Our whole journey had taken about a month. When we got to Dr. Kaufman's house, it was late, and Mrs. Kaufman with her newborn baby, Karolyn, was ready to go to bed. But we had a wonderful reunion.

Stephen Wang

Bluffton College is like a flower that has blossomed continuously in my heart during the past fifty years. Although Bluffton was not big, it was tidy, peaceful, and beautiful. I truly loved the people of Bluffton.

James Liu

Dr. Kaufman first took us to the home of Dr. Mosiman, president of Bluffton College. We also met some of the teachers. Stephen and I walked around the campus and tried to get acquainted with the new place. Before the term began, we did some cleaning work on the campus.

Stephen Wang

To earn money for expenses, I pruned trees and cared for the campus lawn. Although I had worked at Yenjing University, I was ashamed to do part-time work, since in China, the intellectuals despised all physical work. At Bluffton, I noticed that many others were working on the campus, and I thought they might be hired workers. When we introduced ourselves, I learned that they were also students. When I found out that American students also did physical work, I felt much better and worked in great delight.

James Liu

At Bluffton, I worked in the kitchen to earn my board. In China, Stephen and I had pooled our money in a single bank account. But at Bluffton, Dr. Kaufman told us, "That is not the American way; you should each have your own account." In the college kitchen, Stephen and I washed caldrons and pans. Sometimes it was hard work because the sweet potatoes stuck to the pans. John Boehr was the cook, and his jokes really amused us. Louisa Yoder, the matron, was a serious woman who acted like a mother. Leora

Mosiman was a jolly girl who wiped the dishes. All of these people helped us a great deal. I surely enjoyed working with them.

Bluffton College: learning the American way

That year, during the fall of 1930, we were registered as juniors. I took courses in social science and German. During the first couple of months I had no trouble understanding the teachers, but I had difficulty expressing myself. When I studied English in China, we had not used idioms. But at Bluffton, the students used slang words and it was hard for me to understand phrases such as *you guys, why in the world, peach of a girl, by gum,* and so on. Sometimes I found it difficult to understand the difference between similar phrases, such as *I think so, I guess so, I suppose so,* and *I imagine so.*

Stephen Wang

We had a few difficulties when we first came to America. I had trouble listening to the lectures, since I was not accustomed to such rapid speaking of English. Fortunately, my classmates helped me with note taking after class. I was able to adjust better by the second semester.

James Liu

On Sundays, Dr. Kaufman usually took us to visit Mennonite churches in Ohio, Indiana, or Illinois, and we spoke to people about the Christian work in China. Sometimes we sang Chinese songs in the churches. We also showed a banner sent by the Chinese Mennonite Christians to the Mennonites in the United States. Its four Chinese characters meant "God's grace is exceedingly great." Sometimes we visited Christian families. This was a way of getting acquainted with more Christian friends and of learning about Christian life in the United States.

Frank Mitchell and John Keller were good friends of mine. When I first went to Bluffton College, I did not know much about the customs of the American people. Frank and John told me many things about the ways of living in the United States. Their room was right next to ours, and I asked them how to act on certain occasions. They explained things patiently and carefully. Frank sometimes took me to different churches in Bluffton. He helped me spiritually. Winfield Fretz and Bill Huttenlocher were good friends of mine, too. Winfield often corrected me when I used the wrong words. I respected him as my teacher. I often took walks with them on the campus or to the college farm. One day Winfield,

Bill, and I passed an iron bridge on the way to the farm. Winfield and Bill climbed up to the top of the bridge and I took a picture of them with Winfield's camera. That picture always reminds me of our friendship.

Stephen Wang

We lived in Lincoln Hall. We were the only students from the Far East in the whole school and were conspicuous, but everyone was friendly to us. The one who left the deepest impression on me was the president, Dr. S. K. Mosiman. Professor Herbert W. Berky also influenced me, since I learned chemistry from him. He was a patient teacher and had a profound knowledge of his subject. I liked sports and often watched football, basketball, and baseball games, so I learned to know Coach Andrew C. Burcky.

On weekends, John Keller often went home to Lima, Ohio, on the interurban railroad. James and I went to Lima several times with him and learned much about the American social environment. Another friend, Gerald "Chip" Kriebel, was amusing and cheerful. Harry Yoder, with whom I sang in our Glee Club, had the gift of eloquence. I also recall singing with Henry Detweiler and Homer Clemens.

James Liu

The Glee Club made a great impression on me. Professor Russell A. Lantz was the director and he was strict with us, but also kind. Fortunately, I could join the Glee Club. I learned quite a few pieces of music during our trips to several midwestern states. One time we sang at a broadcasting station in Chicago. It was quite an experience for me, one of the big thrills of my life. I surely enjoyed my school life during the year at Bluffton College.

James Liu

After the 1931 spring term, Dr. Kaufman accepted a position to become vice president of Bethel College in North Newton, Kansas. When the summer vacation began, Dr. Kaufman took his family, Stephen, and me to Bethel College by car.

Stephen Wang

Along the way, Mrs. Kaufman sometimes drove the car to let him rest for awhile. The farther west we drove, the more wheat fields we saw. We learned that Kansas, the main state for producing wheat, was called the "granary of America." This interested us, because our native provinces also produced wheat.

James Liu

After three days we got to Moundridge, Kansas, Dr. Kaufman's hometown. People there were really kind to us. The next day, Dr. Kaufman took us to Bethel College. The Kaufman family stayed on the first floor of Goerz Hall and we stayed upstairs. While at Bethel, I suffered from malaria, but Dr. A. M. Lohrentz gave me some medicine and I soon recovered.

Bethel College: a promise to keep

When the summer term began, I took Europe Since 1870, History of Education, Child Psychology, and Culture. In the latter course, Dr. Kaufman compared world cultures. It was very interesting. When the fall term began, I registered as a senior. Besides my regular studies, I worked two to three hours every day except Sundays trimming trees, cleaning the windows of the school buildings, and cutting grass on the campus.

Stephen Wang

Newton was a larger town than Bluffton. When we arrived at Bethel College, we adapted quickly. We could speak English fluently. Occasionally, we went to the grocery store to buy vegetables and flavorings, and then prepared Chinese food to entertain the Kaufman family and other friends.

Dr. Kaufman's brother and parents lived in the country, not far from Newton, and they invited James and me to visit for a few days to see an American farming operation. We were surprised to learn that all the land around the farm belonged to this one family. Dr. Kaufman's brother invited us to watch them reap the wheat. This was the first time we had seen tractors and harvesters.

James Liu

During our year at Bethel College we visited Mennonites in Kansas, Oklahoma, Nebraska, Minnesota, South Dakota, and North Dakota.

Stephen Wang

I worked in the Science Hall laboratory every Saturday afternoon. The lab was at the south end of the second floor; next door was the women's dormitory. Once, I went to open the window and saw some girls washing and cutting their hair and lying prone in the sunshine. I was surprised and asked them what they were doing. They replied that they were getting ready for dating in the evening, and asked whether Chinese girls did this. I told them that Chinese girls did not.

At Bethel, I was deeply impressed with Dr. J. W. Kliewer, the college president. Professor P. J. Wedel was a good chemistry teacher, strict and scrupulous. Professor J. H. Doell of biology was a serious and earnest person. I really liked him. Of my classmates, Albert Gaeddert, our class president, was active in sports and music. Another of my friends, A. Theodore Mueller, was a good soccer player and also a capable leader.

Our mission school, Hua Mei, had closed after Dr. Kaufman left China. Already while we were at Porter High School, James and I had discussed this and had decided that in order to set the school up again, we should divide the work. Thus, James studied social sciences and I studied natural sciences. At Yenjing, James had specialized in sociology and I in chemistry and biology. At Bluffton and Bethel, we both took education and elective courses. I knew that I must return to Kaizhou to live with my mother in her remaining years. James and I both knew that E. G. Kaufman had used a great deal of his energy and painstaking care to establish Hua Mei High School. James and I had promised Dr. Kaufman that when we went back to Kaizhou we would reestablish Hua Mei High School.

James and I promised Dr. Kaufman that when we went back to Kaizhou we would reestablish Hua Mei High School: graduation, Bethel College, 1932.

I decided to promote friendship between the people of the United States and the people of China: graduation, Bethel College, 1932.

James Liu

At the end of May 1932, our commencement was held in the town hall of Newton. All of our classmates received bachelor's degrees. President Kliewer made an encouraging and inspiring speech. A few days later, the college held a farewell meeting for Stephen and me in the same building. The hall was crowded to the doors. Each of us gave a speech. I talked about how I had gotten acquainted with many Americans. In conclusion, I quoted Romans 8:31-38. I surely appreciated what these American friends had done for me during our stay in the United States. Praise the Lord.

Leaving America during the Great Depression

During the summer of 1932, Dr. Kaufman sent us to the Iliff School of Theology in Denver. First, however, we went to the summer YMCA retreat at Estes Park, which lasted ten days. Martha Unrau and three other Bethel schoolmates went along with us. Many Christians from different states attended the meetings. There were Bible discussion groups, prayer meetings, and recreational activities. We heard many inspiring speeches and enjoyed learning to know many new friends. Estes Park is a beautiful place.

After the retreat, we went on to Iliff. I took Christian Ethics and Methods of Preaching. I also took two courses at Denver University, Educational Psychology and Political Science, under Dean Duncan. He was a good teacher. We stayed there until the end of August, when Dr. and Mrs. Kaufman came to Denver and took us around the city. The next day, we returned to Bethel College.

The Great Depression made it difficult for Dr. Kaufman to get funds for our school expenses, so Stephen and I decided to return to China. My two-year stay in the United States meant a lot to me. I learned many things spiritually and intellectually. I appreciated what my American friends did for me, especially the teachers at Bluffton and Bethel. At that time, I decided to promote the friendship between the people of the United States and the people of China. I wanted to bring cordial greetings from the Mennonite Christians in the United States back to my Chinese Mennonite friends.

Stephen Wang

As we prepared to leave America in the autumn of 1932, we saw California vineyards and orchards abandoned by growers because the fruit was too expensive to transport to market. We saw rotting figs, oranges, and other fruits; a sight truly inconceivable to the Chinese because in China a bumper crop would have made the peasants very cheerful.

At San Francisco, we boarded the ocean liner *Roosevelt* [James recalls it as the *Herbert Hoover*]. Along the way we stopped in Hawaii, where James and I bought some pineapples, and then we continued the journey to Yokohama, Japan. I met a fellow Chinese passenger who asked me how I could believe in God and science at the same time. One of my expectations upon going to America had been that I might discover a conflict between science and religious faith. During my years there, however, I found that not only that they did not conflict, but that my religious faith grew as I saw the results of science. I told the Chinese passenger that I knew that this big ship moving peacefully over the great sea to a definite goal did not follow its course without a hand at the helm guiding and directing it. I also knew from the experience of my own life that our universe with its purpose did not follow its course without an unseen Hand guiding and directing it. Faith in God had taken deep root in my heart and no one could take it away, even in the later, chaotic, years of my life.

Part III. The approaching storm: 1931-1937

1931. Japan seizes Manchuria (Northeast Provinces); Chiang decides not to resist the Japanese until after he crushes the Communists.

1934-1935. Long March of Communists to the northwest. Hitler comes to power in Germany.

1936. Mission celebrates twenty-fifth anniversary; membership of church is 1,175. Wilhelminia Kuyf arrives.

1937. Japan invades China; Nationalists and Communists form a united front to fight Japanese; Nationalists move capital west to Chongging; Japanese "Rape of Nanjing."

While James Liu and Stephen Wang studied in America, Japan invaded China and took possession of the productive Northeast Provinces (Manchuria). Chiang Kai-shek turned his back on the invaders and directed his military energies to eradicate the pockets of Communist insurgency within. The two young men returned to positions of leadership in a China soon to be engulfed by war.

Mission-church relationships were strained. Chinese leaders were asking for more authority in the church, and the mission was pressing the young church to assume more financial responsibility for operating the schools and hospital. Finally, in 1935, a joint committee submitted a constitution which was approved. Despite the 1927 evacuation of missionaries, economic depression, war,

At the twenty-fifth anniversary celebration of the mission, James spoke on Anabaptist history and Stephen spoke of disentangling the Christian gospel from Western structures: Kaizhou, April 26–May 3, 1936.

and mission-church tensions, church membership had grown to 1,175 by 1936. At the twenty-fifth anniversary celebration of the mission, James Liu spoke on Anabaptist history and Stephen Wang spoke of disentangling the Christian gospel from Western structures.

Meanwhile, in diverse areas of China, a civil war became more intense. In 1934, surrounded by Nationalist forces, ninety thousand Communist troops broke out of their Jiangxi-Fujian (Kiangsi-Fukien) base and marched six thousand miles northwest to Shaanxi Province. In fourteen years, Mao Tse-tung and his colleagues of the Long March would move from a village headquarters in Shaanxi to Beijing to rule all of China.

On the night of July 7, 1937, a shot fired at Marco Polo Bridge outside Beijing erupted into war between China and Japan. Thus began the Pacific sector of World War II. On February 11, 1939, Japanese troops occupied Kaizhou.

4. High school principal finds a wife
James Liu

After graduating from Bethel College in 1932, I went back to the General Conference Mennonite Mission at Kaizhou, my hometown, and took a position as principal at the mission's Hua Mei High School. I remained there until 1946.

When I returned to the mission school, it was limited to one year of junior high. Each year we added more classes, and the school grew rapidly. By 1937, the enrollment was 250. The elementary school, attached to the junior high, had an enrollment of 300.

Love the Lord Society conducted daily evening prayers, evangelistic work, and organized a committee to aid new students: Principal Liu, center in back row.

The courses we offered were prepared by the education department of the Nationalist government, and we also offered Bible courses. Besides school work, I also took an active part in church and mission work.

During this period, the Nationalist Guomindang troops fought with the Communist Red Army in Jiangxi (Kiangsi) Province. Finally, the Red Army carried out the Long March, a major strategic movement of the Chinese workers and peasants. The Red Army succeeded in reaching the revolutionary base at Yenan in northern Shaanxi Province after crossing eleven provinces and covering 12,500 kilometers during 1934-35.

Bomb in a basket on the train to Manchuria

In the summer of 1933, a retreat was to be held at Beidaiho (Peitaiho), a resort city in Manchuria on the Bohai Gulf, which I planned to attend. When I got to Beijing, a train was ready to leave for Manchuria for the first time in two years, since the Japanese army had occupied Manchuria. On that day, July 1, 1933, the train from Beijing to Manchuria started up again. I got on the train. When it arrived at Tienjin, a Communist got on with a bomb in a basket. He sat in the car behind the locomotive and put his basket under the seat. When the train got to the next station, the Communist got off the train.

I was sitting in that same car, back near the door. A young man and young lady came into our car, and I said to the lady, "Sit on my seat and I will find another place to sit." She replied, "Thank you, but I will try to find a seat in the front." Finally, she and her brother found the empty seat where the bomb was hidden.

When the train got close to Tang-gu station, the bomb exploded. The lady's legs were blown off and she died after losing too much blood. The young man's head was injured and he was rushed to a hospital. When I got to Beidaiho, I found out that the young man and young lady had also been coming to attend the summer retreat. Their father, a faithful Christian, was the head of the department of finance of Honan Province. The young man was a college graduate and worked in a bank in Shanghai, and the young lady had been a student at Nanjing University. The Communists had bombed the train because they disapproved of resuming ties with Manchuria, which was under the control of the Japanese imperialists.

I was grateful to God that the young lady did not take my seat. If she had taken my seat and I had taken hers, I might have been bombed. I did not know what would happen. Thank the Lord.

In the fall of 1934, we invited Stephen Wang, his wife Rui-ling, and his brother Wang Hsien-chang to teach in our school. They helped a great deal in teaching, discipline, and athletics. In 1937, unfortunately, all of them left. We were sorry to see them go—it was a great loss for our mission.

Because of the increased number of students, accommodations were insufficient and the mission needed additional buildings. We erected twelve new rooms to be used as the student dining room, kitchen, storeroom, and workers' quarters. The former kitchen and dining room were turned into dormitory rooms.

We had many student organizations, but the one that was most helpful was Ai Chu Tuan (Love the Lord Society), with more than one hundred boys and girls. They conducted daily evening prayers, Bible study classes, weekly devotional services, evangelistic work, and organized a committee to aid new students. On Sundays, the students went to church, Sunday school, and Christian Endeavor.

One of my students during the Kaizhou years was Yang-Gian-kuei, now a retired vice minister of the Department of Weapons of the State Council. In 1987, he came to the Beijing railway station with two chauffeured cars when Bert and Rhoda Lind and my son Timothy and I visited the capital city. We were guests in his home, which was once the residence of the British counsel. He is gifted in Chinese calligraphy and his wife is an accomplished gardener. Only recently did I learn that he was a Communist party member when, fifty years ago, he enrolled in our Mennonite high school. At the time, the government school had refused him admission.

God saved me through Hazel

Hazel T. Yang was born in Huahsien, Henan Province, on September 7, 1911. This was the year of the founding of the Chinese Republic and the General Conference Mennonite Mission. The name of Hazel's village was Yangtsun. She grew up in a poor family. Her grandfather, a teacher in a mission school for girls, died in the fall of 1937. Her grandmother was blind. Her father was Yang Qi-zhou, a Chinese doctor. He died following the Chinese liberation of 1949. Her mother, Tsuei Hsun, was an uneducated woman. She died in Hengyang (Heng-yang), Hunan Province, on March 8, 1963.

Hazel was the only daughter of her parents. She attended the mission girls' school and graduated from junior high school in 1928. For the next two years she taught in the mission girls' primary school in Kaizhou. Then she attended Yu Jen School of Nursing in Kaizhou and graduated in 1934. Hazel excelled as a

I went to see Hazel, but all the nurses opposed my visits: wedding of James and Hazel, with Stephen and Margaret as attendants, H. J. Brown as minister.

nursing student. During the national unified examination for graduation, she got the highest mark in her class.

In 1933, Hazel and I served together on the Christian Endeavor committee at our church. After we learned to know each other, we met together quite often. But we could not be very open about our friendship. When people saw us, they said, "Look at that, two young people—a young girl, a young man—talking together in public. They shouldn't do that." I didn't care, because I loved Hazel. We began writing to each other so people wouldn't talk. But we didn't mail the letters. There was a nice old woman, a friend, who carried our letters back and forth to each other. We did this for a year and became engaged. Dr. C. L. Pannabecker, superintendent of the mission hospital, told me, "You picked the best girl of our nursing school."

In the spring of 1934, Hazel got pleurisy. That summer, she had to stay in the hospital. I went to see her, but all the nurses opposed my visits, saying "You are one of the leaders of the mission. You should wait until you get married." But I told them that I had come because she was sick. I told them that I had come to sympathize with the patient, not because I loved her. Really, I loved her very much.

We were married on November 25, 1934. Rev. H. J. Brown officiated at our simple wedding ceremony. We did not buy anything for each other. After the ceremony, we served a tea party with five Chinese yuan (one dollar of American money), which we received from Rev. Samuel J. Goering as a wedding gift. We also invited my grandma to join our wedding meal.

At that time my monthly pay was twenty-seven Chinese yuan and I had to feed a family of nine members, three yuan each. After we were married, Hazel's mother came to live with us. Other members of our family lived with us, too: my parents; my two brothers, Peter and Amos; a girl cousin who attended the mission school; and a boy from a poor family who also attended the school. Our living standard was low. Later, the mission decided that because we had a big family, they should increase my salary. Then I received about thirty-five yuan a month, and our living conditions were better.

For nine years, Hazel was ill and could not work. In the fall of 1943, she began teaching biology in Hua Mei High School and served as the school nurse.

In the summer of 1945, I got acute pneumonia. The mission hospital was closed because of the Japanese invasion. Hazel tried very hard to buy medicine from private clinics. She took good care of me and slept on the floor beside my bed. She was not only a nurse but a good doctor. Finally, I was healed; God saved me through Hazel.

She took an active part in church work. She was chairwoman of Christian Endeavor and the Women's Association, and served as Sunday school teacher and organist.

5. A promise to open the mission school
Stephen Wang

During our journey home from America, I met an American girl of Chinese origin, Li Xue-ming. She was going to China to see her sister and brother-in-law. Li's father was a merchant in San Francisco. We got together day after day on the ocean liner and gradually came to love each other.

Li had graduated from a college in San Francisco, and had never been to China. Her habits and ways of living were those of an American. When we got to Shanghai, we were full of contradictions. She asked me what I would do when I got to Kaizhou. I told her that I would probably work in a church or a church school. She asked me to come with her to Guangzhou (Canton) and said that perhaps her brother-in-law could find a teaching position for me. But I told her that I must go to Kaizhou to see my mother and brothers. I didn't take her with me because I was afraid that she wouldn't be able to adapt to the environment at Kaizhou. We finally decided that we would part, temporarily. Before we said good-bye to each other, she gave me a photograph to keep as a souvenir.

In Shanghai and Nanjing, James and I joined a patriotic organization that sought to save the country through education, industry, and Christianity. Most of its members were college graduates. By that time, I had developed the ideal of saving my country through Christianity plus education. I believed that China was poor, weak, and backward because so many people didn't believe in Jesus Christ. Government officials and warlords indulged in foolishness and failed to engage in honest work. If everyone could believe in Jesus Christ, I thought, they would abide by the law and the nation would gradually become peaceful and prosperous.

We tried unsuccessfully to obtain a piece of land from the Henan provincial government to build a new rural center for developing our ideals. We then went to Kaizhou by train. All of the people in the church met us warmly, and we felt a strong sense of responsibility. We expressed our heartfelt thanks to those who had helped us in the long journey to America. After reaching Kaizhou, we soon became so busy with mission work that we gave up our work with the patriotic Christian organization.

Teaching and preaching in Damingfu

When I returned to China in the autumn of 1932, James and I discussed how to reopen Hua Mei High School. We decided that James would stay at Kaizhou and I would work with Samuel Goering and Aganetha Fast at Damingfu, one of the six areas where the General Conference Mennonite Church in China had a mission station. Daming was a seat of government that controlled many counties, including Kaizhou. I went there with my mother to help the two missionaries gain a greater command of the Chinese language.

Our language is difficult to learn and even more difficult to use correctly. Many missionaries could hardly speak it, and when they did, they often made fools of themselves. Rev. Peter Boehr's Mandarin was fairly good, but one time in Kaizhou, while he was explaining his surname, he said something in Chinese that to our ears was a swear word. His slip caused an instant response and the whole room rocked with laughter. A missionary whose work is to preach the gospel to the masses must master the language.

I was also assigned to work in the church, Sunday school, and Bible class. I often assisted an evangelist, Zhang Jing, by giving sermons. Young people from the two normal schools in Daming often came to hear my sermons. Sometimes I went to the countryside to preach, carrying my mother on my bicycle.

In Daming, I was responsible for youth work, and I went to the schools to get acquainted with teachers and students. Through our visits, I found that many of them were interested in studying English. With the consent of the Mennonite missionaries, I opened an English class. About forty teachers attended, and I introduced them to the ways of the church and the doctrines of Christianity. Some of them became devoted Christians. I also gave private lessons to the children of a local government official and became a friend of the family. The official helped to create better conditions for our mission work.

Finding a wife in the circle of the church

While I was in Daming and had stable work, I began to think about marriage. I was twenty-eight years old, and had to go about it slowly. First, I had to find a girl in the circle of the church. I had just arrived and knew only that there were not many single Christian women. Second, I had to find a young woman who would be gentle, kind, and good-natured, because after our marriage we would have to live with my mother, who had an impetuous and impatient disposition. In traditional Chinese family life, one of the usual difficulties was the relationship between a young married woman and her mother-in-law.

I knew several young women, but either they were not Christian, or I was afraid they would not get along with my mother. I was corresponding with Li Xue-ming, whom I had met on the steamship, but I felt that she could hardly live in this environment.

In Daming, I often visited a clinic operated by a man named Dr. Zhang. One day Dr. Zhang came to my home and told me that he wished to introduce a young woman to me. Her name was Zhang Rui-ling, and she was from a Christian family of Chengan County, Hebei Province, about thirty miles from Daming. Her parents were peasants, although her father later became a cotton merchant. She was the eldest of seven children, and attended church schools. Muzhen Girls' Senior High School, where she had graduated in 1931, was one of the best schools in Beijing. In the

I knew several young women, but either they were not Christian, or I was afraid they would not get along with my mother: wedding of Stephen and Margaret at Daming in 1934.

spring of 1932, she became principal of the only girls' primary school in Chengan, her home county.

Dr. Zhang acted as a matchmaker; he told me that she would satisfy my conditions. She was well educated (a woman graduate from a senior high school was hard to come by, especially a graduate of a famous school in Beijing). She was a Christian and came from a Christian family. She was gentle, kind, and good-natured. He spoke to me just like a matchmaker would have, emphasizing her strong points but not talking about her defects.

In order to find out the facts, I went to Chengan three times. I made inquiries about her from a woman whom I knew well, and she told me almost the same things about Zhang Rui-ling. On a second trip, I asked some other friends about her. They, too, told me the same things. Back in Daming, I told Aganetha Fast what I had been doing. She told me that she wanted to help me to understand Zhang Rui-ling, and she went to Chengan County with me to see her personally. We rode thirty miles on our bicycles. She visited the girls' primary school for two days and talked with Zhang Rui-ling. Then she told me the same things I had already heard, and suggested that I go see Rui-ling myself. I met her the next day and we got acquainted. That was during the middle of

December, and I asked her to visit me during the New Year's holiday. She came to Daming and we were engaged.

Shortly afterward, I received letters from two young women whom I had known from my high school days. Both wanted to know whether I was married. I immediately wrote to them about my engagement, and I also sent the pictures of my former friends to my new fiancee.

We were married on July 13, 1934. Our Christian wedding was less elaborate than a Chinese non-Christian wedding might have been. Before the ceremony, William and Matilda Voth drove their car to Chengan to bring Zhang Rui-ling and her parents to Daming. Zhang Jing, the pastor of our church, was the chief witness of our ceremony. The church was full of people, including our families and members of my English class. After the ceremony, I entertained the guests, who presented gifts to us. Aganetha Fast had left Daming to go to America on furlough, so my bride (Margaret) and I lived briefly in Miss Fast's home.

Teaching at Kaizhou was a family affair

During my year of work at Daming, I never forgot James' and my promise to Dr. Kaufman to reopen the mission school at Kaizhou, and Margaret and I went to Kaizhou after our marriage. James and I wanted to introduce many of the things we had learned at Bluffton and Bethel to the school in Kaizhou. For instance, students did all kinds of miscellaneous work around the school in order to earn money. We also enjoyed training the students in an all-around way—morally, intellectually, and physically—as we had been taught in the American schools. This was different than the system of education in old China, where my father, a typical scholar, had suffered from poor health and had been ignorant of all daily affairs. We wanted our students to develop fully.

We decided to enroll new students from outside the church. The tuition they paid helped to ease the school's financial difficulties. Among the new students was a group I had recruited from the Daming area. We hired three new teachers with competency in mathematics, languages, and history. One of these, Bai Yun-xue, became a good Christian soon after his arrival. I was fortunate to learn some Japanese from him.

James served as the school's principal and taught English. I served as academic dean and taught chemistry, physics, and biology, and my wife taught arithmetic and algebra. One of my brothers taught physiology and physical education. Margaret was dean of girls and my brother was dean of boys. A year later, my second brother joined the faculty; during that year, four members of my family taught in Hua Mei High School.

Margaret, the only woman teacher in the school, treated the girls kindly, so they often visited our home on the weekends. All of us had a great deal of contact with each other, not only through the classroom, but also in daily life and in sports events and other activities. As the leaders of a church institution, we had the grave responsibility of helping the students to become devoted Christians. We persuaded them to attend religious services on Sundays. The students performed choral works or presented plays on Christmas and Easter. Many of our students became evangelistic workers and teachers.

Some of our students were politically minded. One of the girls, Wei Xiu-zhi, left the school in 1937 and joined the guerrillas against the Japanese and Guomindang and later died in Rumania on a mission of the Chinese Communist party.

Another student eventually became the vice minister of the Fifth Industry Department of the central government. He was already a Communist when he came to our school, having just been expelled by his previous school. As the dean of Hua Mei school, I knew him to be a good young man—tall, popular, a well-

We trained the students in an all-around way—morally, intellectually, and physically—as we had been taught in the American schools: tennis team with Coach Wang (far left).

disciplined student and sportsman. After graduating from Hua Mei in 1937, he joined the guerrillas, in the Taihang mountains, who were fighting for Chinese liberation against the Japanese invaders and the Guomindang army. Following the war, he went to Russia to study industry. He returned to direct a factory that produced heavy machinery, and later, he took the vice ministry position in Beijing.

Many of our students have enjoyed success in their chosen fields. During the Cultural Revolution, many of them suffered all kinds of hardships and calamities, but most of them held firmly to the truth of Christianity. A man named Guo Lan-tian is a good example. Although he suffered political persecution, he believed firmly in the Lord, and today he is the representative of the Christian church in Daming city.

Part IV. Two wars at once: 1937-1951

1937. Sino-Japanese War begins.

1938. Albert and Wilma Lichti Jantzen and Etta Davis arrive.

1939. Japanese troops occupy Kaizhou. Marvin and Frieda Albrecht Dirks arrive.

1940. James Liu elected chairperson of the new church conference.

1941. Pearl Harbor; United States and Allies (with the exception of the U.S.S.R.) declare war on Japan. Chennault organizes American Volunteer Corps ("Flying Tigers"). In April, eight missionaries remain after evacuation of married women and children. Marie Regier and Elizabeth Goertz interned in Japanese concentration camp in Shandong Province; three missionary families interned in the Philippines.

1941-44. Stalemated war against Japan; Chiang sets up military cordon around Communist base in Northwest China.

1942. China-Burma-India Theater of War established with Chiang Kai-shek as commander in chief and Lt. General Joseph W. Stilwell as chief of staff.

1944. Chiang forces resignation of Stilwell.

1945. End of war; Japan defeated.

1946. Collapse of United States efforts to bring Nationalists and Communists together in a coalition. Mennonite Central Committee begins relief work along Huang Ho River with centers in Zhengzhou and Kaifeng.

1946-49. Civil war; Nationalists retreat and Communists expand.

1947. MCC headquarters move from Kaifeng to Shanghai.

1949. Communists capture Beijing. On October 1, Mao proclaims People's Republic of China; Nationalists flee to Taiwan.

1951. P. J. and Frieda Sprunger Boehr leave Sichuan. Frank Beahn, last MCC worker, leaves China.

With the outbreak of the Sino-Japanese War, the stories of James Liu and Stephen Wang divide. China moved westward. Chiang Kai-shek established his new capital far up the Yangtse River to Chongqing in the western province of Sichuan. The Japanese slaughter of thousands in Nanjing, called the Rape of Nanjing, spurred the migration westward. Stephen's story is akin to that of hundreds of thousands of Chinese students and teachers who moved west in flight from the Japanese armies.

Some remained longer, as did James, but by the war's end, in 1945 he, too, moved on—southward to Kaifeng and Zhengzhou where he joined the Mennonite Central Committee relief teams. In 1948, he moved much farther south to Hengyang. Like millions of other Chinese, these two men were uprooted and swept along by war to distant places.

At first, the war brought little injury or disruption to the church. Seventeen missionaries attended the annual mission conference in late 1940. In April 1941, women and children were evacuated, leaving eight missionaries in the program. Church membership had nearly doubled between 1935 and 1940, reaching a total of 2,273 members. Anti-Western feeling appeared to subside. Chinese replaced missionaries in positions of leadership: Dr. Paul Hu at the hospital and Chang Ching in the Bible school. In 1940, the first five Chinese pastors were ordained. A new church conference, with elected Chinese officials, assumed responsibilities held previously by the missionaries. James Liu was elected conference chairman.

James Juhnke says, "This Chinese Mennonite Church in 1941 was stronger and more independent than any of the General Conference mission churches of that time." One might add, "of *any* Mennonite mission church of that time."

With the American declaration of war against Japan on December 8, 1941, the remaining missionaries were soon interned: Marie Regier and Elizabeth Goertz in a concentration camp in Shandong Province and three missionary families in the Philippines.

At first, the war brought little disruption; seventeen missionaries attended the annual conference at Kaizhou in the fall of 1940: (left to right, front to back): Wilma Jantzen with Lyman and Grace, Aganetha Fast, Philipp Ewert, Maria Brown, Elizabeth Goertz, Sylvia Pannabecker, Lelia Pannabecker with Donald and Daniel, Irene Ewert, Alice Ruth and Anita Pannabecker, Ralph and David Ewert, Betty Jean Pannabecker, Wilhelmina Kuyf, C. Lloyd Pannabecker, Marie J. Regier, Etta Davis, Martha Ewert, Frieda Dirks with Marvin Jr., August Ewert with Martha, Albert Jantzen, H. J. Brown, S. Floyd Pannabecker, Marvin Dirks.

The war years in China, 1941-45, is a story of corruption and ineptitude. Barbara Tuchman in *The Stilwell Diaries* and Theodore White's *In Search of History* describe the decline and fall of Chiang and the Guomindang during and after the war.

In 1945, the Mennonite Central Committee entered this war-torn country to aid the refugees along the lower Huang Ho River and to engage in agricultural rehabilitation. From 1945 to 1950, thirty-nine MCC volunteers worked in twenty-one projects in China. Often, their status was precarious since they worked in areas contested both by Guomindang and Communist troops. China was falling apart.

When the last MCC workers and missionaries left in 1951, a curtain descended between the church in China and the church in North America. Those who had been friends for thirty years could no longer write or visit. Silence.

6. On the road to Kaifeng, a word from God

James Liu

On July 7, 1937, the Anti-Japanese War began. Early in 1938, Japanese troops came close to Kaizhou. The Japanese soldiers stole from and killed many people. They also raped the young Chinese women. The Japanese soldiers made a lot of trouble for our mission. Since all the missionaries had left the city, most of the Chinese workers and their families moved to Tung-ming station on the south side of the Yellow River.

After awhile, Rev. Floyd Pannabecker and Dr. Lloyd Pannabecker came back to Kaizhou and some Chinese workers came with them from Tung-ming county. At that time, more than a thousand refugees had taken shelter in the school and in other parts of the mission compound. I began doing refugee work.

At that time, there were different groups of soldiers: Nationalists, Japanese, Communists, local military, and bandits. Various soldiers came to our school and tried to find out what we were doing. Each group wanted something from us. It was difficult to deal with them. I had to be careful; if I misspoke one word, they would say that I was against them and worked for other groups. When the Japanese army occupied Nanjing, three hundred thousand people were killed. When the army occupied Chang-Yuan (site of a Mennonite mission station), soldiers forced two thousand people to line up in fields and then they shot them with machine guns.

One of our former students, Liang Wen-hua, was a Communist who worked in the Kaizhou area. One day his father came to see him and said that he wanted to stay in our school for the night. I told him he had better not, because the Japanese often inspected the school. I sent him to a friend in the countryside. That very night, the Japanese officials inspected every place within the school grounds but did not find evidence that we were harboring Communists.

During the Japanese occupation of northern China, nearly all the schools were closed. The junior high students who had graduated had no chance to go on to school; so, in 1939, we introduced a senior high and added one class each year. The students realized that under these conditions, they were fortunate to have an opportunity to attend school, and they worked hard.

Kaizhou's Christians carry on after Pearl Harbor

Since other schools were closed, many college graduate teachers were unemployed and we were able to hire good teachers. We had well-qualified teachers for every course. The mission turned over its kindergarten to Hua Mei High School, so our school had both an attached kindergarten and elementary school. We continued to offer regular courses issued by the government in addition to Bible courses and religious worship services.

The Pearl Harbor incident occurred on December 8, 1941. By then, Kaizhou had only two Mennonite missionaries, Miss Marie J. Regier and Miss Elizabeth D. Goertz. On the day of Pearl Harbor, Japanese soldiers detained the two women and took them to the Catholic church in Hsin-Hsiang, Henan Province. They were held there and later were brought back to their house where two policemen guarded them.

At first, the police watched them closely. No Chinese workers were allowed to see or talk to them. After awhile, some Chinese Christians talked pleasantly to the policemen and gave them some tokens of kindly feelings. The Christians were then allowed to visit the two missionary women. When Miss Regier and Miss Goertz needed something, the Chinese Christians did their best to provide for them.

Finally, the Japanese sent the women to Beijing. Years later I read the book *In Japanese Hands*, by Henry J. Brown, and learned that Miss Regier was in a Japanese internment camp. After that, I did not hear anything about them. Rev. and Mrs. Brown were also detained in Daming for some time and then were sent to Beijing. Then, they went to the Japanese camp in Wei-hsien, Shandong Province.

After the Japanese attacked Pearl Harbor, a Japanese official asked us to close the school because he wanted the students to do propaganda work. I spent two days persuading him to let the students go home. Before the students left, our teachers decided to let the third year senior high students graduate a semester early.

In early 1942, Japanese officials wanted me to turn over the mission property. I said, "I have no right to do that." They replied: "You are the chairman of the General Committee. You have the right to do that." I told them again: "I am only one member of the General Committee, not the whole body. I simply cannot do it." When I refused to sign, they became very angry.

After the Pearl Harbor incident, the Christians of Kaizhou still carried on church work. They had worship services on Sunday and used the offering to pay the pastor. Some country churches held Sunday meetings, too. After 1944, the Christians had worship services in private homes.

If I misspoke one word, the soldiers would say that I was against them and worked for other groups: Japanese army officers with S. F. Pannabecker at his Kaizhou home.

The Japanese leave Kaizhou

In 1942, the Japanese soldiers left Kaizhou. A group of Nationalist army men working for the Japanese came to Kaizhou. Our junior high school reopened, but there was no mission fund. The school was supported by the tuition of the students and we sold newspapers and old books which the missionaries had left in order to pay part of the school expenses. The teachers received no pay, only their board. The local government ran the elementary school.

Meanwhile, on August 21, 1944, our son Timothy was born. We hired a nursemaid for him. In the fall of 1944, Kaizhou was liberated. I asked the Kaizhou Perfectural Commissioner to take over the school, but he refused because the situation of Kaizhou was not quite in order. The administrative office of the Henan-Hebei-Shandong border region supported the school with a certain amount of money to repair the school buildings. They also sent several teachers and a vice principal to us.

Because I did not know the policy of the People's Government (local Communist government), I was afraid. So in the spring of 1946, Hazel and I left Kaizhou for Kaifeng, the capital of Henan (Honan) Province. We did not take anything with us.

On the first night of our trip, we stayed in a Christian home.

Changchun

Shenyang

Beijing

Tianjin

Kaizhou

Lanzhou

Kaifeng

Huang (Yellow)

Zhengzhou

Xi'an

Nanjing

Shanghai

Chengdu

Chang Jiang (Yangtze)

Chongqing

Hengyang

Kunming

Guangzhou (Canton)

HONG KONG

.... STEPHEN WANG —·—·— JAMES LIU
— — — THE LONG MARCH

During the night, the Lord said to me, "Forgetting what lies behind and straining forward to what lies ahead" (Phil. 3:13). I heard it plainly. We had not liked leaving Kaizhou because we had worked for the mission for fifteen years. Our relatives and friends were there. We had felt badly about it. When I heard the words of the Lord, I felt full of energy and confidence.

7. Crossing the Yellow River to flee the war
Stephen Wang

During summer vacation in 1937, our family traveled to my wife's home, Chengan County in southern Henan Province. Margaret and I had two sons, Jian-jing and Jian-wen. We traveled by horse-drawn carriage from Kaizhou to Qingfeng, Nano, and Daming; then took a bus to Chengan. The whole trip took about three days.

At the end of August, we had planned to return to the school, but the Zhang River flooded after a big rain. I was also suffering from a foot disability and had trouble walking. I wrote to James that I could not return to school on time. A few days later, the Japanese invaders came from the north to Handan, a railway station not far from Chengan. Our family decided to go south across the Yellow River to flee the calamity. We expected to return to Kaizhou after the Sino-Japanese War, which we thought couldn't last very long.

Family scattered by Japanese invaders

We took our elder son, Jian-jing with us, but left Jian-wen with Margaret's parents. Her parents asked us to take their two sons and two younger daughters with us. Margaret's parents were unprepared to leave their family property, and our younger son suffered an illness and needed to be sheltered from the wind. So they stayed behind. In the meantime, I wrote to my brothers and asked them to bring our mother to Zhengzhou, where we would meet them.

We reached Ci-xian, the nearest railway station, where all the trains were full of wounded soldiers. The station was small, but many refugees crowded in, fleeing for their lives. When a train arrived, everyone pushed and squeezed to get on. All the cars were loaded with wounded soldiers. Sometimes the car roofs were full of people.

We thought we had no opportunity to get on a train. But while we were waiting, I entered a freight car filled with wounded and dead soldiers. I quickly called to my wife and her brothers and sisters to board the car. By the time the guard discovered that we had all gotten on, the train began to move. In this way, we were able to go south.

During part of our trip south, for a distance of about fifteen miles, I sat on the front of the engine because there was no room elsewhere.

We arrived at Xin-xiang, a station on the northern side of the Yellow River. It was daybreak, and everyone was hungry and thirsty. Fortunately, a benefactor handed out millet gruel at the station. My wife's brothers and sisters were bashful, but I went to get some gruel for all of us. The train departed again, and when we reached the bridge of the Yellow River, people called out in happy astonishment because they had never seen it before.

When we reached the Zhengzhou station, we met my brothers and sister-in-law, but learned that my mother had not joined them. She thought that the Japanese invaders would not come to Wang Tun because it was too small a village. During our absence in the following years, however, she suffered greatly. In 1938-39, heavy rains flooded the village for several months. All the others fled and became beggars; my mother was left alone in the village. She

We expected to return to Kaizhou after the Sino-Japanese War, which we thought couldn't last very long: Margaret and Stephen with Jian-wen and Jian-jing in 1937.

caught fish from the flood waters and cooked it without salt. Finally, my father-in-law went to Wang Tun and took my mother to stay at Chengan.

Those of us who met at Zhengzhou stayed together in the station because we could not find an inn. As refugees, we had few means of earning money. I gave my brother Hong-zhang five dollars to go out on his own and sent him to Kaifeng. There, at a school for military officers, he told people that he had a brother who had returned from America and who had many friends in government. He told me in a letter that he then took an entrance examination and, in a group of several hundred candidates, received the third highest score.

Life and death in Xuchang

The rest of our family went on to Xuchang, the first large station south of Zhengzhou. We rented a house in the city, gathered edible herbs and ate sparingly. Due to the indefinite duration of the war, I felt it important that my younger family members find work. We couldn't sit idly and use up all our money. My brother, Xian-Zhang, had some medical knowledge, and I introduced him to a military friend. My brother and his wife became medical officers in an anti-Japanese campaign and worked on the front lines.

My wife's brothers and sisters were young. I tried to find a school for them in the southwestern part of Henan Province. Most of the schools in the area were closed due to the war. Some schools had been moved from the war zone. The education department of the Central Government of Guomindang took in students who became separated from their families during the war. Margaret's brothers and sisters all attended and graduated from the National First Senior High School at Shang-ji. The government paid for their education.

Only my wife, son, and I remained in our small dwelling in Xuchang. Although we had left Kaizhou, we had not left God and the church. We lived near a church and found many friends there. Pastor Xu and the missionaries asked me to help them with refugee work. I organized the young people into a Bible class and choir. Sometimes I gave sermons. There was also a theological school in the city. I was invited to work there, but declined because I thought the Japanese invaders would cross the Yellow River and come to Xuchang sooner or later.

One day, a guest came to our home and my little boy, Jian-jing, was not obedient. He disturbed my visit with the guest, and I became very angry. I spanked him and put him in a dark room and locked the door. He cried in the room and said: "I know I am wrong, Papa. I correct my errors." He tried to get out but the door was locked. He wept loudly and was afraid.

The next day he fell ill. In wartime, it was difficult to find a doctor. I found a doctor of traditional Chinese medicine. He said that my little boy was suffering from meningitis. Although we were able to get medicine for him, a few days later my little boy died. At about the same time, we received a message that our second child, Jian-wen, had died of diarrhea. In the meantime, my brother, Hong-zhang, sent us some children's clothes and toys. He never expected that his little nephews would die before we received the parcel.

A Chinese proverb says that misfortune never comes singly. A few weeks later I got a letter from a friend, saying that Hong-zhang, who had been in the school for military officers, had died of peritonitis and had been buried at Yi-chang, Hebei Province.

After the death of my children and younger brother, I was deeply grieved. My wife wept all day at the grave of my boy. We decided to go south to Xinyang to see a friend of my wife's. At the same time, I received a letter of appointment to become a staff member of the Xinyang Normal Senior High School. So in the spring of 1938, we left Xuchang.

Bombed nearly every day in Xinyang

Margaret's friend in Xinyang, Liu Yanzhou, was a native of that city and had married an army officer. They helped us very much during our time there. The city had a population of about two hundred thousand people, and was situated in the southernmost part of Henan Province. The weather was hot and humid in the summer.

I had known the principal of Xinyang Normal High School, Zhou Shaoyan, from my years at Kaizhou. He asked me to teach English in the junior high and physics in the senior high. I soon learned to know and enjoy the teachers of the school. A few weeks after we got to Xinyang, we had a third son.

Japanese airplanes bombed Xinyang nearly every day, and we ran for shelter. The school decided to move fifteen miles out of the city into the mountainous countryside. Chinese schools frequently moved to the rear during warfare. When the Japanese invaders came to northern China, many schools moved to abandoned temples. If there was not an available temple, the school rented houses or constructed simple buildings.

My wife and I walked to the new location. When we got there, our baby was very ill. The school doctor, Fan Yong-kan, provided medicine and our child soon recovered.

We then received notice from the education department of the provincial government that our school had to move far away to the southwestern part of Henan Province. We returned to the city and discovered that our school had been bombed. Some of the buildings were destroyed, and one person had died.

Mud tables and benches in the temple

Our school moved 250 miles west to Shigang, a market town of about two hundred households. Family members of the school's faculty went by bus, while students and teachers walked. The students were organized into teams or groups; I led a team that acted as an advance party. The roads were muddy. We had to keep going, however, because of the continuing air raids.

Gradually the students tired. Sometimes we found old temples to stay in during the cool nights. We gathered branches and sat around the fire. We ate a hot meal each evening; during the day we ate cold bread and salted vegetables or pickles. In order to raise the students' spirits, I often told stories from the Bible, such as the birth and death of Jesus Christ and the events of his life, including the miracles.

When we arrived in Shigang, my wife and son were already there. Rev. Chang was the minister of a small church in the town. I met him, explained that I was a Christian, and asked him to help me find a place to set up our home. He told me of a thatched cottage just behind the church. The church was close to our college, and I often went there in the evenings. On market days, when peasants came to the town from all around, Rev. Chang preached the gospel. I took charge of the religious services on Sundays. We worked well together.

Xinyang Normal High School was reorganized in an old, damaged temple. We had no platforms, tables, or chairs in the classrooms, but we made mud tables and benches. In the winter, the temple was cold, so we plastered paper over the windows. We had a difficult time. We had only one small coal stove, and sometimes it got so cold that students could not hold their pencils. On warmer days, we sometimes held our classes in the open air.

In the summer of 1939 in Shigang, we had a sorrowful experience, the death of our third son. One day the Japanese bombers came and we ran with our baby into the wilderness to escape the bombs. It was a hot day and we brought along some watermelon for our baby. But after he ate the watermelon, he began to have diarrhea and then he got dysentery. We had an inexperienced doctor at the school who was unable to get medicine, and our baby died. Within two years our three children had died, so we were deeply grieved. Soon afterward, my younger brother and his wife came to Shigang, as did my wife's friend Liu Yanzhou and her husband. We all lived together and I didn't feel as lonely.

In the spring of 1940 we had another baby, a daughter, Alice.

Chemistry classes in a mountain market town

In May 1940, I went to Henan University to teach a graduate course in chemistry. Henan University was the only institution of higher learning in Henan Province prior to liberation. It had four colleges: Literature, Science, Agriculture, and Medicine. Students from Henan Province who passed the entrance examinations boarded at the university. I had been to the university, located in Kaifeng, several times in 1922-23, during my high school year there. During the war of resistance against Japan, the school moved from Kaifeng to Zhen-ping, a county seat of the southwestern part of Henan Province. The school then moved to Tantou, a market town thirty miles farther west.

Tantou was a town with about two thousand residents, located deep in the mountains of Songshan. It was difficult to reach, with only a narrow mountain pass. I had been afraid that I would not do well as an instructor there, since I had not used chemistry or English for several years. But many of my friends at Shigang persuaded me to try, and I went to Tantou alone. My family planned to join me during summer vacation.

When I arrived in Tantou, I had about a week to prepare, and then I lectured in English to students for the next two months until the semester ended. During the summer, the school sent someone to Shigang, and to a nearby town, Xixiakon, to get my family and the family of another professor. Margaret and five-month-old Alice rode on a sedan chair and arrived in Tantou after a five-day trip.

The administrative offices of the university school were located in a courtyard of a landlord, and classes were held in a temple outside the town. The president of the school was an old scholar who was a good friend of the local warlord. Although the president knew much about ancient Chinese culture, he thought little of modern education or of the natural sciences. The members of the secretariat were also old scholars. The private secretary of one was practically a government spy who kept a close watch on the words and deeds of the faculty members and students. If he found persons who resented the school or government, he promptly ordered the army or police to arrest them. The dean of Lecture Training supervised behavior at the school. At that time, the Communist party and the Guomindang were hostile political powers, and the schools of the Guomindang government did not allow communism to flourish. So the dean of Lecture Training had the task of insuring that students and faculty did not become Communists.

All of the deans and most of the professors were natives of Henan Province. I, too, was a native, but had lived there for only six years. I left Henan University in 1942 because I thought it was not safe. I believed that the Japanese invaders would come sooner or later. The invaders did come to Tantou in 1944, and the school staff and students had to flee.

Rebel students return to their books

After leaving Henan University, I went to assist a friend, Liu Zi-qian, who was having difficulties as the principal of Kaifeng Girls' High School. Some of the students there, whom I had taught three years earlier at Xinyang Normal School, had begun an uprising. I agreed to go to Xi-chuan to try to resolve the conflict.

When I arrived, I met with some of the students to learn about the source of agitation. The students suspected that the principal's brother-in-law, an employee of the school, did not have the school accounts in order. They also believed that the principal himself was an incompetent administrator and had protected his corrupt relative.

The students leading the protests were in the senior class. All of them hoped to enter a college or university after the summer. I told them: "In order to meet the entrance examination of a university, you have to obtain a diploma from this school. If you continue to agitate, you will lose the opportunity to pursue your education. I plan to go to Chenggu to teach in the Northwestern Teacher's College and I hope that some of you can also go to Chenggu. I advise you to stop the agitation and to begin preparing for your entrance examinations."

Before I left, I arranged for the dismissal of the brother-in-law and spoke with the principal about the charges against him. The agitation gradually ended.

I went on to Chenggu to the Northwestern Teacher's College and six months later my wife and two daughters joined me. Northwestern Teacher's College was formerly called Beijing Normal University. At the beginning of the war of resistance against Japan, many educational institutions moved to Chenggu. This particular school relocated outside the city walls.

Chenggu had a population of about ten thousand. The climate was comparatively warm and damp, much like that of southern China. Our family, however, had always lived in northern China, and we had difficulty adapting. We often fell ill. Our eldest daughter, Alice, suffered from an inflammation of the spinal cord. I took her to a hospital in Luo-yang, but the doctor said that there was no cure. She could not hold chopsticks or stand up. When we returned to Chenggu, I found a traditional Chinese doctor. After several months of taking traditional medicine, Alice gradually recovered.

Soy sauce factory supplies four schools

During the summer of 1943, the school decided to move to Lanzhou (Lan-chou) where it already had a branch. I had two choices. The school's administrators hoped I would go to Lanzhou to head the department of physics and chemistry. I also had the option of going to Shan-tai, Sichuan (Szechuan) Province, to teach at Northeastern University. I decided to go to Lanzhou because its climate was similar to that of northern China. So we moved by automobile in mid-1943. It took three days to complete the 350-mile journey. The dirt roads were rough, and everyone was tired when we arrived at Lanzhou.

Lanzhou, with a population of three hundred thousand, was the capital of Gansu (Kansu) Province. It was an important city in northwest China. The city had several minority peoples, including Hui, Mongol, and Tibetan. Our school relocated in a suburb of Lanzhou city, with buildings consisting of sun-dried mud brick and straw. There was no water source close by, so people used donkeys to bring in water from the Yellow River. For light we used kerosene lamps. Lanzhou had a Christian church, and every Sunday we went by carriage to services.

Many of the professors who headed departments had studied in America, Germany, or France. I headed the department of chemistry and physics from 1943 to 1950. Our department had six professors, five lecturers, and four assistants. We also had several part-time teachers.

I sometimes held two or three teaching jobs concurrently at Northwestern Teacher's College, Lanzhou University, and Northwestern Agricultural College. In addition to the teaching work, I set up a soy sauce factory with two other men, Mr. Sheng and Mr. Liu, and we produced soy sauce for one university and three colleges. We used the following raw materials: soybeans, wheat bran, salt, and syrup. My interest in this enterprise and in a nearby flour mill (which used the water of the Yellow River) was related to my longtime ideal of reviving China through religion, education, and industry.

During the war of resistance against Japan, the Japanese frequently bombed the city, so the Lanzhou Guomindang government decided to establish a Central Committee of Technical Air Defense. I became a member and occasionally gave lectures on air defense techniques and on the design of air raid shelters. Later, during the Cultural Revolution, these activities caused me trouble.

Making the long move to Manchuria

In 1945, the Chinese won the war of resistance against Japan. The first thing I did after the victory was to send my brother back home to get my mother. A few months later she came to Lanzhou and lived with us for the next sixteen years. After our marriage, I had learned of my wife's many distinguishing merits. She easily handled routine matters in our family as well as the relationship with my mother.

During the years between the victory of the war of resistance against Japan (1945) and liberation (1949), paper currency depreciated rapidly. Everyone tried to obtain silver dollars. We had a difficult time during those years.

Before liberation, we were ignorant about the Communist party of China. The Guomindang government fabricated a story that the Communists were all bandits who committed murder, arson, and every crime imaginable. The government called Mao Tse-tung (Mao Zedong) the bandit chieftain. Thus, the landlords, capitalists, and reactionaries were afraid of the Communists. Many people who had overseas relatives fled abroad prior to liberation.

In 1949, when the Chinese People's Liberation Army came near Lanzhou, my family moved temporarily to Lanzhou University where my sister-in-law was teaching in an attached primary school. On September 22, 1949, the army attacked the city. The war lasted only a day and a night. The following morning, the city was liberated. For several days, all the people went out to parade in the streets. Everyone carried flags and banners and beat drums and gongs to greet liberation. The teaching and administrative staffs of all the colleges and universities went out to join the celebration.

The liberation of Lanzhou was the beginning of a new epoch in my life. I found out that the Communist party of China and all its armies were not as bad as the Guomindang government had propagated. On the contrary, they were nice people. Their style of life and work was honest. They were courteous and polite toward the masses. I surely had a good impression of them at first.

After liberation, the Department of Education of the Guomindang government declared that Beijing Normal University would reopen. The president of the school asked me to go to Beijing to help start the school, but I refused because my two daughters and three sons, born between 1940 and 1948, were too small to make that difficult trip.

I took a sabbatical in 1949-50. I wanted to travel to other places, but that was impossible because of the war of liberation. I directed an experimental center of industrial research in Lanzhou and in the summer of 1950 led the graduates on a research trip to Xian (Sian). I then sent them back to Lanzhou but decided not to return there.

Although Lanzhou had a good climate and was a safe place to live, it was rather backward in culture. Its living standards lagged behind. My children had never seen a train or a presentable building. I had debated for a long time whether or not to leave this out-of-the-way mountain area. When, during the summer of 1950, I was offered an opportunity to go to Zhangchun (Changchun), I no longer wavered. I went to our former home at Henan to visit relatives, and wrote to my wife to bring our children and my mother to Henan. In the late summer of 1950, we began the long journey from Henan Province to Zhangchun, Jilin (Kirin) Province, Manchuria, where I would teach at Northeastern Normal University.

8. Five years with Mennonite Central Committee

James Liu

Before we left Kaizhou, we had heard about the work of the Mennonite Central Committee in Zhengzhou (Chengchou) from Rev. Wang Wan-chu. When we got there, we met Rev. S. F. Pannabecker, the director of MCC. In Zhengzhou, we stayed in the Free Methodist mission.

One Saturday, Pastor Liu of the Free Methodist church asked me to preach on Sunday. During that night, the Lord said to me, "Work hard for the Lord." I was much encouraged by the Lord's words. Early the next morning I prepared my speech on "working

We became regular workers for the Mennonite Central Committee for the next five years: James and Hazel with Timothy in 1947.

hard for the Lord." So I preached on that topic, and felt comfortable. Rev. Pannabecker asked us to work with MCC. Two months later, the headquarters of MCC moved east down the Yellow River to Kaifeng, Henan Province. We became regular workers for MCC for the next five years.

Working with MCC after the Yellow River flood

When we left Kaizhou in 1946, our son was only twenty-one months old. About a month later, he came to Kaifeng with my mother. In Kaifeng, Hazel taught Timothy 128 Chinese characters. At the same time, I introduced him to some English expressions, which he picked up quickly. The MCC members enjoyed being with him.

While we worked for MCC, Hazel was in charge of a country clinic and at the same time conducted a clinic in Kaifeng city. During our two years in Kaifeng, Hazel trained a girl named Kuo Chi-jung to be a nurse. I spent most of my time as an interpreter, and sometimes I worked in the office doing translations.

During this time, MCC brought relief to the flooded area in Henan Province. Many, many poor people needed food and clothing, bedding, and grain. Their homes had been flooded by the Yellow River. We helped them with temporary relief supplies. We also made cotton loans to the poor people, giving them a certain amount of cotton to make cloth and getting back a small amount of cloth. In this way, people were able to work and obtain cloth. We also did relief work in Zhengzhou, Qi-Hsien, Zhu Hsien Zhen, Fu Kou, and other places. Some of the MCC workers were assigned to hospitals in Changsha, Guangzhou, and Anyang.

Dr. Hu, one of the four Mennonite doctors who worked for MCC, is the only one of the four now living. He is eighty-five years old and walks with a cane. He suffered a great deal during the Cultural Revolution.

In late 1947, the headquarters of MCC moved to Shanghai because the situation in Kaifeng was tense. We began working in the southern part of China in Jiangxi and Hunan provinces. At that time, an orphanage in Hengyang, Hunan Province, was run by the local relief committee. The municipality wanted to be relieved of responsibility but wanted to retain jurisdiction. We insisted on complete control. We spent six weeks hammering out a contract before MCC agreed to take it over. In the spring of 1948, Wilbert Lind (whose Chinese name was Lin Hwei-be), Ku Yin-ting (Theodore), and Hazel and I traveled by boat and train to Hengyang in Hunan Province to take charge of the orphanage. I have lived in Hengyang ever since.

Saving the lives of Hengyang's orphans

When we arrived, there were 250 orphans who had lost their families in the Anti-Japanese War. The youngest orphans were about two or three years old and the oldest was about fifteen. Timothy, age three, came with us to Hengyang, and studied with the deaf-mute orphans under Hazel's direction. We organized the orphans age six and over into a primary school of six grades. The next year, we added the first grade of junior middle school and sent the graduates to other schools. About ten local teachers served in the primary school. The children attended school a half day and worked a half day. Mr. Ku was the business manager, Mr. Lind was in charge of the children's daily life, and I was in charge of educational work. Other MCC workers included Aaron and Marie Herr and Glenn Graber.

In addition to the courses authorized by the government, we taught Bible classes. Every morning we had worship services and Mr. Ku led the meetings. Each semester there was a catechism class. In 1948 and 1949, Rev. Henry J. Brown and Pastor Li Pei-yu baptized fifteen orphans.

The daily routine of the orphanage was well supervised. Wilbert Lind was really a hard worker. He took good care of the children and studied the Chinese language. At meals and bedtime, he watched over the children and attended to their needs. He spoke good Chinese and was well liked by the children, who called him Uncle Lind.

In recent years, many of the orphans have said that had it not been for MCC, they would not be alive today. Most of them had been beggars on the streets of Hengyang and surrounding villages. Many lived by lying and stealing. Each day the government sent trucks to give them each a bowl of porridge. They had no school; they were hungry, cold, and dispirited. When MCC took over, the children received three balanced meals a day and padded cotton winter suits.

In 1948, Hazel became director of the Hengyang orphanage clinic. There were 146 orphans who had favus on their heads. This skin disease caused by a fungus is difficult to cure, but Hazel did her best to take care of the children. Finally, all recovered but one.

After liberation, Hazel was transferred to the fourth hospital in Hengyang. In the winter of 1952, she began her work in the hospital. She became the head nurse of the outpatient department. She was a hard worker. Dr. Zi, superintendent of the hospital, said: "Hazel can do the work of two persons. She is a many-sided person." Sometimes she gave lectures to all the nurses and sometimes she served as a doctor when there was a shortage.

Shortly before liberation, Rev. Brown wrote to us from Shanghai and asked us to take up mission work there. Hazel said, firmly: "We cannot bear to leave the orphans alone here because no one will be left to take care of them. The Lord wants us to stay with the orphans." We stayed.

Children in peril from flood and war

During the Anti-Japanese War, the Japanese soldiers and the Guomindang troops fought in Hengyang for forty-eight days. The Japanese airplanes bombed Hengyang and destroyed most of the buildings. In June 1949, again fearing war, we decided to move the orphanage to the countryside. One hundred and thirty-nine orphans went to live with distant relatives. With the remaining 111 orphans, we hired eleven boats, loaded our blankets, food, bags of salt, and sailed.

During the first night we were caught in a downpour. The river overflowed its banks. The boatmen moored the boats on the side of a mountain. When we stayed there, we saw that many houses had toppled down. The bodies of dead people and animals floated down the river. We heard people stranded in trees or on buildings shouting loudly and calling for rescuers to save them. How miserable they were!

During the heavy rains, one of our nurses carried a six-month-old baby to a farmer's house on the bank. Soon the water came into the house. Half an hour later the house was full of water. The nurse went upstairs. Another half hour later, the house had nearly collapsed, and the nurse shouted for a boat. One of our boats sailed to the house and rescued them. We stayed on the mountain for four days, until the flood subsided. Then our boats sailed on and another four days later we reached Hong Lo Miao. The distance from Hengyang to Hong Lo Miao was only thirty-five miles but it had taken us ten days to get there.

One day in September, the liberation army suddenly began shooting from the mountainside near the orphanage. The Guomindang troops began to shoot back. Our orphanage was right in the middle of the battlefield! We asked the captain of the Guomindang soldiers to slow down the shooting because we wanted to leave to find a safe place. But they thought we were family members of the liberation army's soldiers, and they wanted to kill all of us. We begged them not to, and explained that the children were orphans. Finally, they let us leave the battlefield and we found a big temple to stay in. I carried a lame girl on my back and pulled two children with my hands. Thank the Lord, not one child was lost.

But we lost everything else. The children returned to Hengyang with only the clothing on their backs. The Hengyang Presbyterian church and others contributed some food. I went to Shanghai and obtained two bales of clothing and blankets from MCC worker Frank Beahn.

After Hengyang was liberated, we returned to the city. In 1950, I went to Hong Kong and got some funds from another relief unit to keep the orphanage going. On January 5, 1951, the Hengyang government took over the orphanage. We were so happy because we did not have enough money to feed the children. In 1953, I was transferred to the First High School in Hengyang and Hazel was transferred to the city's Fourth Hospital. Theodore Ku was assigned to teach in a primary school ten miles away in the country. A year later, in April 1954, he died. About eight years later, the government discontinued the orphanage. Today the building still stands, but is hardly recognizable since being renovated as a factory.

Orphans now productive workers and worthy witnesses

I often wondered what happened to the boys and girls who eventually left the orphanage. When Bert and Rhoda Lind visited China in February and March 1987, we met twenty-seven of our orphans. From these and from others who had visited me earlier, we gleaned the following information about ninety orphans:

Twenty-six are skilled and semiskilled workers, including three deaf and mute who went to Canton (Guangzhou) to learn sign language. Eleven are college graduates and four have finished Bible school. Three are medical doctors and five are nurses. Nine are in government positions and two are government cadres (officials). One is a high naval officer in Tingtau. One former orphan is now director of the Public Safety Bureau, Hengyang, one of the highest paid positions in the city.

Farmers number three as do bank employees. Two are druggists and two are miners. Four blind orphans went to Shanghai to learn Braille and are now all working in that city. One blind fortune teller who went to Shanghai to learn Braille was later dismissed.

Others found work as a commercial department section chief, photographer, manager of a store, an excellent cook in a large restaurant, manager of a large warehouse that supplies department stores, radio announcer, agricultural researcher, vice manager for an international shipping firm, and postal worker.

One migrated to America about ten years ago but a few were less fortunate. Two died as soldiers in the Korean War and one became insane and was expelled from the army for antigovernment expression.

Bert wrote comments on a number of these visits, many of which were in homes where we were served meals. The orphans were so happy after thirty-eight years to see "Uncle Lind" and to meet his wife Rhoda, whom they met for the first time. From Bert's journal:

•A woman was in prison for five years during the Cultural Revolution. A government official had come to Hengyang and asked her, "What is Christianity? Who is a Christian?" When he learned she had identified with Americans as a child in the orphanage, he imprisoned her. She is a happy Christian.

•Two women related how as children they were beggars on the street eking out an existence. They never dreamed one day they would have a comfortable home, a good job with sufficient income, and desirable clothing. They are extremely happy. Both are neatly dressed. One, a nurse, told how the Japanese army robbed her family. Her mother and brothers starved to death. She and her grandmother went begging, and after her grandmother died, she was sent to two different orphanages. Her eyes became infected with trachoma; someone suggested she be sent to a hospital, but the organization refused; she is now blind in one eye. During the Cultural Revolution she was required to sweep streets wearing a sign that read "Reactionary Missionary," since she had been in the MCC orphanage.

•As two men reminisced, they began to laugh and sing in Chinese, "When we all get together how happy we'll be." They had learned this song in the orphanage years ago.

•One orphan was age three when MCC arrived. She was eight when Hazel and James Liu left, and she remembers a Christmas play with shepherds. She is now forty-four and has a sixteen-year-old daughter in high school. The woman is an inspector in an electric cable factory and her husband is a chief engineer, responsible for one thousand workers.

•One man told of an orphan who is a high official in a county office. He decided to visit this official and as he entered the door, the official leaned back in his chair in a proud manner and asked, "And what do you want me to do for you?" He told him he was not asking for any service, and walked away.

•A man, who is a party member, informed his staff that he was planning that afternoon to visit an old teacher from the United States whom he had known years ago. His staff encouraged him to visit us.

•One evening two deaf and mute women, who learned sign language in Canton, came to visit. They returned the next evening with another deaf orphan and his wife. They stayed for two hours. They are retired, in good health, and very happy. One wore a beautiful sweater that she had knitted; Hazel Liu had taught her to knit.

•We visited a retired woman who with her family lives in a three-room apartment on the fifth floor of a building. She was excited to see us and served tea and cookies. She had been unaware of our coming, but her home was neat. This former orphan, once a beggar, lived exceptionally well. The family had an electric washing machine, treadle sewing machine, radio, color TV, recorder, flush toilet, and electric heater. It seems incredible. Up another flight of stairs lived a deaf and mute person in a larger apartment. It is the Chinese custom to show guests the house; it was immaculate. Here we were offered tea and oranges.

Flight from China halted

Getting reacquainted with some of the orphans has been most interesting. Bert and I enjoyed reminiscing about our experiences together in MCC. Bert told the story of a 1948 unit meeting in

Shanghai. The personnel, who had been working in Henan Province in northern China, had just been evacuated by airlift to Shanghai. At this meeting, they debated whether or not to move the program to South China (where MCC might have to leave again as a result of Communist advances), or whether to enter Taiwan or return home. Unit morale was low. As Bert told it:

There was a tense discussion after which one person made a motion that the China unit close up and return home. The motion was entertained without a second for some time until James Liu rose to his feet and pled passionately that in no case should the unit evacuate from China. He said that during his visit to the United States some years ago he had found Americans to be hard workers who still maintained the pioneer spirit of adventure and did not easily give up when faced with opposition and difficulty. He went on to say he was quite disappointed that these characteristics were not more visible in the meeting. He added, "Forget the fact that you are Christians, even Americans as I know them would not flee from this situation." After he was seated, the one who had made the motion immediately withdrew it and the spirit of the meeting changed dramatically. It was agreed that the unit would attempt to work in South China and in Taiwan.

Part V. The years after liberation: 1949-1987

1950. Korean War begins; Chinese troops cross the Yalu to fight Americans.

1953. Korean War ends; some U.S. troops remain in South Korea.

1955. Mao Tse-tung orders collectivization of farms.

1956-1957. During the Hundred Flowers campaign, six weeks of criticisms are voiced; the critics are punished.

1958. Mao initiates the Great Leap Forward, an effort to decentralize industrial production, and organizes the country into communes.

1959. Tibetan uprising brings reprisals from Beijing and results in the flight of Dalai Lama.

1960. Soviets withdraw aid and technicians from China; China and Soviet Union disagree over appropriate road to communism.

1962. Border warfare between China and India.

1963. Rival armies are positioned along the Soviet-Chinese border.

1966. Mao proclaims Great Proletarian Cultural Revolution to rekindle revolutionary fervor.

1967. China explodes its first hydrogen bomb.

1971. American Ping-Pong team visits China; Henry Kissinger makes secret trip to Beijing.

1972. President Nixon visits China and issues Shanghai Communique: "There is but one China and Taiwan is a part of

China"; United States agrees to "progressively reduce its forces and military installations in Taiwan."

1976. Cultural Revolution officially ends; Mao dies; Gang of Four (led by Mao's widow) arrested; extreme leftists and moderates struggle for power.

1977-78. Deng Xiaoping emerges as preeminent leader.

1979. U.S. and People's Republic of China establish diplomatic relations.

1982. Under moderate leadership of Deng Xiaoping, Communist party approves new party constitution that breaks with radicalism of Mao. Mennonite groups organize China Educational Exchange to place teachers in Sichuan, Shenyang, and other parts of China and to receive teachers and students in North American institutions.

On October 1, 1949, in Tiananmen Square, Beijing, Mao Tse-tung proclaimed the People's Republic of China. A toxin of pride coursed through the Chinese. Their leader heralded them as a people "who had stood up." Not all viewed that October 1 as liberation. For those who had hoped that a Nationalist party victory would usher in an era of independence and progress, the triumph of Mao was "the fall of China."

Essential to an understanding of world events since World War II is the China story. One traces monumental changes: from the Long March to the social experimentation of the early Mao years, to the Great Proletarian Cultural Revolution, to the cult of Mao and then his death, to the emergence of the moderate, pragmatic leadership of Deng Xiaoping with the four modernizations: agriculture, science, industry, and military.

During the early 1970s, as the Cultural Revolution began to ebb and as China-Soviet hostility intensified, the Chinese cautiously opened a door of friendship to the West. As the first friendship groups visited the People's Republic of China, many returned to the West to praise an idyllic peasant paradise. Others reported critically of oppression during the Cultural Revolution. Gradually, the shadow and the light, the multisided complexity of China came into perspective.

As Chinese-American relations were restored, James Liu and Stephen Wang, who were thought to have died, were able to make contact with American friends and with each other. The two sons of Mennonite mission in these intertwined autobiographies now contribute their unique perspectives to the years from 1949 to the present.

Meanwhile, North American Mennonites have returned to China, not as missionaries but as teachers, doctors, nurses, and agriculturalists in the inter-Mennonite China Educational Exchange program. Replicating the model of James Liu and Stephen Wang studying in America fifty years ago, the Chinese now send teachers and scholars to North American communities to learn and to share of their experiences. A new day of reciprocity has begun.

9. Jailed in my own school
James Liu

After liberation, I taught English in a Hengyang high school. In 1954, English teaching was not allowed in schools because of the Korean War. At that time, China had friendly relations with Russia, so I taught the Russian language instead. Besides my teaching, I was also a committee member of the labor union of the school. During the Great Leap Forward, our students helped to build factories. Together, the students and teachers carried bricks for the walking tractor plant and the steel rolling mill in Hengyang. The students did not go to class; they only did physical labor. The students also did iron-smelting work. But they were unskilled and many materials were wasted.

The hardships of the early 1960s resulted in great losses for China. But the Chinese people are industrious and have rebuilt our homeland through self-reliance.

Timothy attended school in Hengyang, studied English, and was interested in sports. After graduating from senior high school, he took college entrance examinations but failed. The following year he again failed the exam. Later, I learned that because I had had relations with American missionaries, he was not permitted to go on to college. Timothy decided to go to a vocational school, where he specialized in electricity and graduated in 1965.

Since then, he has worked in Ye Jin Qi Che Xiu Pei Chang factory. He married Hu Lan-xiang (Edna), a middle school teacher. They have two sons. The elder, Paul, was born in 1969 and is in senior high school. The younger, John, was born in 1972 and is in junior high school. They live happily.

In April 1960, I got cirrhosis of the liver and stayed in the hospital for three years. It was incurable, and the doctor told Hazel that I was at the point of death. They ordered a coffin and my mother prepared a burial shroud. I prayed day and night and trusted the Lord to heal my illness. The people's government and the Party were very concerned, and the doctors and nurses gave me the best of care. But my abdominal cavity was full of water. My belly swelled to 115 centimeters. I could hardly sleep. I took all kinds of medicine—Chinese and Western—but did not improve.

In October 1961, a nurse told Hazel about toad powder, a folk prescription. Hazel caught and killed some toads, took out all their internal organs, baked the rest dry and ground it into powder. I took one gram each day. This one gram of powder was divided into three parts and I took one part in the morning, one at noon, and one in the evening. I took the powder for a year and four months, and my liver recovered. Praise the Lord. Finally, the Lord healed me and saved my life.

When I left the hospital at the end of 1962, the doctor told me that I should not go back to work again, because the cirrhosis might recur. So I stayed at home to recuperate. I became extremely hungry for meat, which was scarce and expensive. Hazel bought rats and prepared rat meat for me. I was not told about this until I was well. During the next years, we led a hard life and just ate porridge two times a day. There was a calamity at that time.

Locked up three years by the Cultural Revolution

In the summer of 1966, the Cultural Revolution took hold throughout the country. Red Guards, most of them students, searched homes for things that did not fit the conditions of New China. One day in September, the Red Guards came to our home and took all our things away. They said that all belongings were from the United States, and the United States was the enemy of China. Since I had connections with American missionaries, they considered me the enemy of China.

Hazel's hard work over the years brought poor health to her, and she retired in 1967. On September 18, 1968, I was called into our school by the principal to take part in the Cultural Revolution movement. I was seized and locked up, and endured three years of imprisonment in my own schoolroom. I was severely criticized for being a Christian and an intellectual. For three years, I was not allowed to see Hazel. I was ridiculed and humiliated by students. They said that I was an American spy and a running dog. I was compelled to eat bowls of old cabbage leaves and moldy rice.

When I was in the school, I cleaned toilets. If it was not clean enough, they scolded me. One time the Red Guards asked me to plant vegetables. I had never done that kind of work. If the plants died, the guards scolded me. One day, some Red Guards made me kneel on a bench and they threw snowballs at my face. My eyes were hurt severely. It took a month for them to heal. Another day, when it was very hot, the Red Guards asked the thirteen of us who were prisoners in the school to line up and take off our shoes. Barefoot, we walked downtown. The road was made of pitch. It was very, very hot. My feet were badly hurt and I could not walk for more than a month.

Finally, in July 1971, they could not find fault with me, and they let me go home. When I was released, Hazel told me that she had come to the school to see me, but they had not allowed her to enter. They had told her that I had done bad things that I had never told her about, and that if she didn't return home, they would strike her.

Jiang Qing was the leader of the Gang of Four, also called the Jiang Qing Reactionary Clique. During Jiang Qing's rule, no one was allowed to worship the Lord in public. Christians had to turn in their Bibles, hymnbooks, and other Christian literature, or else destroy them. At first we buried our books, but then we feared that they might discover them. When we finally burned them, we prayed for the Lord to forgive our sins because we had destroyed God's words. We felt badly about it.

During the Cultural Revolution many people were put into prison or were killed. Even some of the old leaders of the central government, such as Liu Shao-Qi, chairman of the People's Republic of China, and General Ho Lung, an outstanding military commander, were killed by the Gang of Four. Finally, in October 1976, the Gang of Four was put under arrest.

In 1976, three great Chinese leaders died. Zhou Enlai (Chou-en-lai), the premier of the State Council, died of cancer on January 8. Zhu De (Chu-teh), commander in chief of the People's Liberation Army, died in July. Chairman Mao Tse-tung died in September. The death of these three leaders was a great loss to our country. The Chinese people mourned deeply. These leaders will always live in the hearts of the Chinese people.

After the Gang of Four, enough to eat

After the death of Premier Zhou Enlai, Hua Guo-feng became the premier of China. Following Chairman Mao Tse-tung's death, Hua Guo-feng became chairman of the Chinese Communist party. Later, Deng Xiaoping (Teng Hsiao-ping) became the great leader. He is outstanding in his ability and integrity. He is amiable and does not want to take the highest position of the central government. He is chairman of the military commission of the Central Committee of the Communist party.

I am glad I did not leave, because now we take pride in our great socialist motherland: Hazel and James, son Timothy and his wife Edna, and grandsons Paul and John in Hengyang in 1980.

In 1978, the Third Plenary Session of the Eleventh Central Committee decided to reform the rural economy. As a result, farmers today not only plant grains but also set up businesses. They can sell their products on the free market in order to earn more money. After four or five years of reform, the farmers' standard of living rose. Quite a few made more than ten thousand yuan. A few farmers bought cars or trucks. Most people now have enough to eat. One hardly sees any beggars on the street.

Scientific methods of growing grain and improving irrigation helped the peasants to increase their products. The output of grain or rice has risen every year. Of course, the first enterprises were connected with farming: a group of peasants set up a roadside market to sell their crops. The entrepreneurs and village collectives have now expanded into all kinds of other enterprises—inns, restaurants, stores, tailor shops, beauty parlors, and light manufacturing. Some entrepreneurs have even opened services in the major cities to recruit maids and other household help for busy urban families. Businessmen can hire workers privately.

In 1985, economic reform began in all of China's cities. Economic reform is continuing smoothly. Our government has also been carrying out the "opening to the outside world" policy, in which foreign friends set up businesses either by themselves or in cooperation with Chinese collectives. In this way, China can use foreign capital and technology to develop its economy.

The mending of the Party is going on throughout the country. The Chinese government is strengthening the socialist legal system. Our government adopts these important measures in order to make the social order smooth going. These are the most important things our new government is doing. Right now our country is stable and united. Many young people have replaced the old leading cadres at all levels. Our government has also raised the positions of the intellectuals.

Retired but still teaching and learning

During the period that I stayed at home to recover from cirrhosis, I was paid sixty yuan (80 percent of my basic salary). I retired in April 1976 and received 50 percent of my basic salary. My length of service was counted from 1951 to 1960 and three years of detention in school during the Cultural Revolution, for a total of thirteen years. In May 1978, a new regulation was issued that if the length of service was more than ten years, the pension should be 60 percent. So I received that amount. In June 1983, I spoke to the mayor of Hengyang about my pension and he said: "Your salary should at least be 70 percent. Beginning next month, you will get that amount." And so I did.

While recovering at home, I did some private work. I had some students who were not good with English and wanted me to help them make up their work. I gave free help to them. Medical doctors from the hospitals of Hengyang often came to my home and asked me to help them in their English reading or grammar. Since my retirement, I have taught English to my two grandsons, Paul and John.

Besides teaching English, I have been quite interested in reading newspapers and magazines. I am also interested in letter writing. Every morning I get up at six o'clock and run or do physical exercises for thirty to forty-five minutes if the weather is good. Sometimes I take a long walk outside of town. Every day I sweep the floors inside and outside the house.

I have two younger brothers. The first is Amos Liu, a pharmacist. He suffers from paralysis and is recuperating at home here in Hengyang. He and his wife are both Christians and they have seven children. My second younger brother, Liu Chung-an (Peter), is also a Christian. After he graduated from college he attended the school of theology at Chengdu, Sichuan Province. He was a pastor in a church in Hsindu County for many years. Now he teaches in one of the high schools in Shandong Province.

Hazel's death and the meaning of her life

After Hazel retired, she took care of the housework that had earlier been done by my mother. She took care of Paul until he was age five and took care of John until he was age seven. She spent most of her time caring for our two grandchildren.

In May 1980, we found out that one of our relatives from Kaizhou was staying in a place eight miles from our home. We were eager to see him, and after a wonderful visit with him, we walked back home. At the time, I was seventy-six years old and Hazel was sixty-nine years old, and she was in poor health. The trip made us very tired. The next day, we asked our relative to come to our home to eat *jiaozi* (dumplings). That day we were busy buying things and making *jiaozi*. In the evening, Hazel was cooking and suddenly fell onto the ground, unconscious. We took her to the hospital right away. She stayed for a week and her health improved. Then she came home, but from that time on her mind was not normal. That day was May 4, 1980.

Edna, Timothy, and I took good care of her and tried to find a hospital for her. The ordinary hospital would not take her, so we took her to a psychiatric hospital. But there the ward was just like a prison. The patients often scolded and hit each other. The doctors suggested that Hazel remain bedfast in our home. A physician came to our home regularly and gave medicine to her. During the first two years, she could recognize people. After that she was less able to recognize people. During the last half year she could not recognize anyone and did not talk at all.

During Hazel's illness, our daughter-in-law Edna took very good care of her. She surely did her best. Edna is just like our own daughter. Timothy tried to get everything Hazel needed.

On August 1, 1984, Hazel suddenly had a high fever. We called the doctor to give her injections. For five days her fever remained high so we took her to the hospital. There the doctors and nurses cared for her, but the fever did not subside. Hazel did not eat anything. In the daytime, Edna took care of her and at night Timothy took care of her. I was there also.

Finally, early in the morning of August 16, she left us and went to heaven. I was glad that she went to heaven, but I have missed her very, very much. Her body was cremated. Hazel wanted it this way—no fuss. We asked our pastor to hold a worship service for her. Hazel was a faithful Christian and a good daughter of our Lord. She was my companion, a constant source of inspiration to me, and a great help in all my work. Hazel, my wife, will live in my heart as long as I live.

After Hazel's death I moved in with Timothy and Edna. I have a room to myself and help with the chores in the home. We are a family. Edna always tells me not to work too hard. She is kind to me. I listen to three daily religious broadcasts on the radio, from Hong Kong, South Korea, and the United States. On my bookshelves are approximately two hundred Chinese and English books. I read three chapters in the Bible each day. I have read to my grandsons in the years since the Cultural Revolution. My grandson John has recently gone to live a thousand miles away with my younger brother, whose wife just died.

My other brother, Amos Liu, a pharmacist, lives with his wife in Hengyang. He worked with MCC at Ch-Hsien-Chen in Honan. He has seven children and fourteen grandchildren who live nearby. He is partially paralyzed and has difficulty hearing. When Bert Lind visited, Amos asked Bert to pray for him. Bert then asked me to repeat John 3:16 in Chinese. This brought tears to Amos's eyes. Amos is keeping the faith.

A return visit to Puyang (Kaizhou)

In February 1985, Timothy and his family went with me on a trip to Puyang (Kaizhou). On our way, we stopped at Zhengzhou, the new capital of Henan Province, to see some former students of our General Conference Mennonite Mission high school. When we arrived at the railway station, they were waiting for us. How happy we were, because we had not seen each other for thirty-nine years. In my mind, they were still boys and girls, but now they are all over fifty years old. They took us by car to a student's home.

The next day was Sunday, and we went to church. When we got there, the big church was crowded. There were about five hundred people in attendance. Praise the Lord, the Christians can hear his gospel again. After church, we were invited for dinner by a former student, Wang Zhih-an. He is working in a movie studio. We had an enjoyable time together.

On the morning of February 11, we went to the place that used to be a Free Methodist Mission middle school. Before liberation, Edwin Schrag and other MCC members taught English in this school. Some of our General Conference Mennonite Mission students attended school here. This place is now a public park. In the evening, we met with a former student who is an actress of the Honan provincial art troupe. We recalled the days of our mission school and had a wonderful visit together. We met seven former students in Zhengzhou, all of whom work in different departments of the Honan provincial government. They entertained us warmly. We surely thanked them for their hospitality.

We also visited Dr. Paul Hu, who was the only Chinese doctor of the General Conference Mennonite Mission. He is eight-five years old and is now retired.

On the morning of February 12, we went to Kaifeng by bus and stayed in a former student's home. In Kaifeng, we visited some former Mennonite pastors—Sung Yun-ting, Liu Jin-O, and Wu Tung-tang. We had prayer meetings in their homes. Some of our former students took us to see the Iron Pagoda, Lung Tin (palace) and the ancient sites of Hsiang Kuo Si built during the Sung Dynasty (A.D. 960-1279). There are two reopened churches in Kaifeng. In addition, there are several home churches. Our former Mennonite pastors often lead Sunday worship services in these places. Usually thirty to fifty people attend.

On February 16, we started for Puyang by bus. When we arrived at Puyang, a former student met us and took us to the reception room of the Puyang Municipality. We talked for a little while and then he took us to our home village, Hua Yuan Tun. When we arrived at our old home, there was a big crowd of people surrounding the car. I could not recognize any of them except my uncle. It seemed to me they were all strangers. Finally, I found out that they were all my relatives. When I had left home in 1946, there were only twelve family members; now there are more than fifty. Most of them were born after I left. My uncle took us to his home and introduced some older ones to us. This was our first reunion since 1946.

The village has changed entirely. There are many new buildings and trees. The standard of living of the people is much higher and they dress better. Most of the homes are equipped with modern furniture. Some of them have radios, televisions, and recorders.

The next day was cold and windy. I took our family to the east suburb where our Mennonite mission compound had been. We came to the former mission high school, Hua Mei. The school yard had not changed much but the doors, windows, and floors of the buildings are getting old and need to be repaired. I told Timothy and his family where Hazel and I used to live, which room was my office, and gave them a brief history of the school. It reminded me of many, many things in the past. This place is now used as a middle school. There are three other middle schools and one normal school around our former mission compound.

The big church building is used as a library by one of the middle schools. The former missionary residences are used as student dormitories or storehouses. The hospital has been enlarged quite a bit and many new buildings have been built. I met a former student who is working in the hospital as the head of the department of obstetrics. It is now run as a community hospital.

One evening two Christian leaders, Rev. Hsieh Shi-shen and Liu Zhung-shan, came to visit. I asked them about the church work in Puyang. They told me that the Three Self Patriotic Movement Committee had been organized. Wang Hsiu-yun, a woman doctor, was elected to head the committee, which consisted of six of our former Mennonite church workers. The department of religion of Puyang had promised to find a place for them to hold worship services. They also promised to return the big church building to the Christians. There are nine preaching places in the Puyang area where the Christians can hold worship services on Sundays. The average attendance of each is from twenty to forty. Young people attend meetings on religious holidays. Each place has a Christian who leads the meeting on Sunday.

Puyang's gratitude for the Christian witness

One day, a local official, Mr. Liu De-yun, came to see me and was very polite. He welcomed me to Puyang and told me that the magistrate of Puyang had wanted to see me before we left the city. On February 23, he returned and said that he would send a car to take us to the city. The next morning we were ready to leave our old home. All of our relatives came out to see us off. They said good-bye to us and asked us to come back again to our beloved old home.

When we got to the office of the magistrate, the chairman of the local People's Congress, the chairman of the local People's Political Consultative Conference, and the first secretary of the Party were all there. The magistrate introduced us to them. We exchanged a few words of greeting with each other. Then the attendant came in and said, "The meal is ready." After a big meal we had a nice visit together. During our conversation, the magistrate said to me: "Your mission and school made great contributions to the Puyang people. Many of your students are working in the government. If you have a chance to go to America again, be sure to tell the missionaries and their children. They can come any time and stay here as long as they wish. They are welcome in Puyang."

That afternoon, the officials took us to look around the oil field. A driver, Mr. Ren, took us to Anyang (sixty miles from Puyang) to the railway station, where we embarked for Hengyang. When we arrived, one of Timothy's friends met us at the station. Praise the Lord! We arrived safely home again.

On this trip we met many old friends, relatives, former co-workers and former students. We saw many places of historic interest. We surely enjoyed the trip. But I felt sorry for the church work in our General Conference Mennonite mission field. No church in our field has been reopened. There is no regular church building for the Christians to hold worship services. We need buildings and Christian leaders very badly.

Pray for the churches in China, please. We have full confidence that God will take care of our churches and give us what we need.

The church in China reaching out

In old China, most of the Chinese churches were operated by a variety of foreign missions. The denominations didn't make much difference to the Chinese Christians, who knew only to believe in Jesus Christ as their Savior. All of the denominations made a great contribution to the Chinese Christians, although some Chinese still think of Christianity as a foreign religion.

After liberation, the Chinese Christian churches were still open. Although the Communists did not believe in religion, they gave people the freedom of religion. After the hardships put upon Christians during the Cultural Revolution, our government again permits us to believe in Christianity. Praise the Lord.

After the founding of the People's Republic of China, the days of the foreign missionaries coming to China were over. Chinese Christians organized the churches. In 1954, the names of all Chinese churches were changed to the Three Self Patriotic Movement Church (self support, self control, and self propagation). There were no different denominations, and we called it the Chinese Protestant Church. Three kinds of committees—national, provincial, and local—operate the Chinese churches.

Some people say that the government runs the church; they say this because of the word *patriotic*, but the Christian must love both the Lord and his own place. Of course, sometimes the government wants to see what is going on in the church. Mennonite people believe in nonresistance. The Bible says if you are compelled to go with someone one mile, you should be ready to go two.

The pastors have to be patient and careful in the matter of government and church relations.

The congregation in Hengyang elected its pastors, who were then approved by the government. This was only a formality, however. Some people think the government runs the church; it does not. The most important question you must ask when people question any government is, "What do they do for the people? How do they care for the people?" I should say that our government has done this quite well during the last ten years.

In large cities and in some smaller ones, churches have been reopened. Christians in rural areas hold worship services in private homes. I do not attend a house church, since Hengyang's church, with more than one hundred members, has reopened. Most of the members are old people. The average attendance on Sunday is from sixty to eighty. Sometimes young people attend the church and sing in the choir. On Easter Sunday, 1985, seven people were baptized. On Christmas Day that year, eight people were baptized. In Hengyang, the total number of church members is more than two thousand. Pastor Ding, a woman, visits me at home about once a month. She asks for my opinions, and I tell her that I have hope for a beautiful future for this church.

In 1985, a friend of mine, pastor Chang Shi-lu, investigated the extent of church work in Chang Yuan, one of five counties in our General Conference Mennonite mission field. He reported that one county had thirty-four preaching places, 2,428 church members with more than 400 attending regularly, one pastor, and twenty-one persons helping with the preaching.

The pastors of our church in Hengyang are trying to reach out to other churches in China and to foreign friends. They are eager to know about the larger church. The cultures of the Chinese and American peoples may be different, but we all belong to one family, the family of God. In Jesus Christ, we are all brothers and sisters. No matter what our nationality or denomination may be, it makes no difference to God.

Once, a Chinese farmer put several bowls of good food before the pictures of his ancestors and asked them to eat the food. An American missionary saw this and asked the farmer, "When will your ancestors eat your food?" The farmer answered, "Well, my ancestors will eat our food when your ancestors smell your flowers in the cemetery." Despite these cultural differences, the Chinese farmer and the American missionary had the same purpose, to show respect to their ancestors.

In our world are many troubled areas. There are also conflicts among different peoples. In Jesus Christ, we have peace in our hearts. God is love and Jesus is the king of peace. We should love each other and help each other. The Chinese church is quite promising, although we are concerned about training new leadership. Some seminaries have been reopened and each year new ones are built. Our pastors in Hengyang, who are old, have invited students in the local colleges and teacher institutes to attend church services, and some do.

In 1985, the Hengyang church sent two students to Wuhan Seminary. The government is willing to cover half the costs of seminary training, but young men who desire to be pastors are scarce.

China cannot print enough Bibles for all those who want them. China is suspicious—with good reason—of Bibles coming in from Hong Kong and Taiwan. It is too bad that so many people do not have copies of the Bible.

Proud to be a Christian in China

How has my personality been formed? My mother was a capable woman. She never went to school, but she knew how to do all kinds of work and learned to read the Bible after age forty. Her way of living had a great influence on me. Another person who helped me was Dr. E. G. Kaufman, my teacher and co-worker. He helped me to know how to love the Lord and serve the people. Dr. Kaufman said, "The chief purpose of work is to glorify God and benefit people." Because of his profound knowledge of social problems, I chose to study sociology and education. During my youth, my mother and Dr. Kaufman influenced me the most.

In 1932, when I returned from the United States and worked in our General Conference Mennonite mission high school, a friend urged me to work for the local government. He said, "You have a big family; you should earn more money to support your family." I told him: "I cannot do that because I am a Christian. God knows our need and he will provide what we need."

When I worked with the Mennonite Central Committee in Kaifeng, a former student, Wang Zhih-Chun, tried to persuade me to teach in Henan University. He said, "Relief work is a tiresome piece of work." I said, "Right now, relief work is more important than teaching in a university because there are so many poor people along the flooded area of the Yellow River. Many of them are dying of hunger. They need food and clothing very badly. I like relief work." He said to me again in a very impolite way, "You are foolish." I told him, "I like to be foolish."

During the Cultural Revolution, I suffered because I was a Christian, and also because I had connections with foreign missionaries. But I am proud to be a Christian. In 1949, shortly before liberation, many Chinese people went abroad. Dale Nebel, director of MCC, asked me whether I would like to go to another country. He said that MCC had work in Taiwan, Indonesia, and the Philippines. If I wanted to go, he would be glad to help me go to any of those places. I told him right away that I wanted to stay in my motherland. I am glad that I did not leave, because now we take pride in our great socialist motherland. I am proud to be a Chinese citizen.

My advice to younger people? It is important to be patient. If something is right, it will become evident gradually. Take time to walk every day. Too many of us run through life. I enjoy time with my grandchildren; it is good to visit and play with them. I can hear well, and I can walk well. I have a family that loves me. I have friends and good memories. I should praise God for all that I have been given.

Finally, I wish to do several things in my remaining years. I want to encourage my grandchildren to really know Jesus Christ as their Savior. But I do not want to push them to be baptized; they must understand the importance of this decision. I want to take an active part in church work. Since Chinese Christians feel a great responsibility to support their churches, I will continue to do my best to keep up the friendship between Chinese Christians and American Mennonite friends. I want to pass on our friendship to the next generation. I will also do my best to contribute to our four modernizations.

10. Labor, the motherland, and peace
Stephen Wang

Changchun (Zhangchun) was the capital of the puppet government of Manchuria before the Chinese won the war of resistance against Japan. While the city was occupied by the Guomindang army, it was besieged by the liberation army. Northeastern Normal University was the only institute of higher learning at Changchun at that time. Its doors and windows had been broken by the army.

When we arrived, much of the city was in ruins. It was a relatively new city, however, and the buildings reminded me of my experiences overseas. I often told my children that if they looked at the style of streets and buildings of Changchun, they would see a city just like one in America.

From 1951 to 1958, Margaret supervised a residential district in Changchun, which had about three hundred faculty families. The university provided a satisfactory dwelling place for our family. The school had eight thousand students and a staff and faculty of about two thousand. The leaders of the school were all revolutionary cadres (government administrators). Many of the professors, including three in our chemistry department, had studied in Russia. During my years at Northeastern Normal University, I taught and supervised research in organic chemistry.

Resisting U. S. aggression in Korea

The liberation of China gave everyone new life. In Changchun, I, too, began to have new life. In the old society, professors had paid little attention to politics. But after liberation, the situation changed and one could no longer separate oneself from political affairs. The ultimate victory of the revolution of the Communist party was not easy. In order to safeguard the victory, the Party launched several political movements, one after another.

The first movement to follow liberation was the war to resist U. S. aggression and aid Korea (1950-53). Everyone from the leaders to the masses joined in. Each day, American bombers flew across the Yalu River to the northeast. Everyone in Changchun ran to air raid shelters during the attacks. The American bombers also dropped gas shells and bacterial shells, so we had to train our students to do gas and bacteria defense work.

My children asked: "Why do the American airplanes come to China to drop bombs and to kill Chinese people? Didn't you tell us that the Americans are friendly and kindhearted people?" I told them that only a small number of government officials and military officers were wrong and bad, and that the majority of the American people were kindhearted and honest. I believed that the Mennonites had not approved of their government's war in Korea. In China, during this time, a movement arose to oppose America. Persons like myself, who had studied in America, were out of luck.

Remolding ideas is long-term work

At the same time (1950-53), another movement arose to suppress counterrevolutionaries. On the eve of liberation, the Guomindang government and senior officials had fled in panic from the mainland to Taiwan. Following this was the movement against the three evils: corruption, waste, and bureaucracy. In 1952, a movement began against the five evils: bribery, tax evasion, theft of state property, cheating on government contracts, and stealing of economic information (as practiced by owners of industrial and commercial enterprises). The government asked the masses to expose persons who had been corrupt in the past. Many embezzlers were denounced in this way, and we called them "tigers" and "beat tigers."

In 1953 began the most important political movement for the intellectuals, the movement of ideological remolding. I had been neither a counterrevolutionary nor a corrupt merchant, so I was not caught in the first several political movements. But I, like most of the intellectuals who had been educated in old China, had bourgeois ideology. In order to fit into the new situation, I had to change over to proletarian ideology.

I had a difficult time during this movement. Every intellectual had to dig out thoughts of bourgeois individualism and selfishness and hand them over to the Party in order to enjoy the confidence of the masses. The goals of the Party were as follows: possess ardent love for the country, serve the people unselfishly, and dedicate one's life for the struggle for communism. Honestly, ideological remolding is long-term work, and one can hardly change one's thoughts completely in a short period of time. But many intellectuals made the adjustment. An old proverb says: "Unless a man looks out for himself, Heaven and Earth will destroy him."

The so-called Great Proletarian Cultural Revolution began in 1966. But beginning in 1957, the antirightist campaign led to several significant events. Because this was a nationwide political movement, no one could escape it. Although I had not come from a landlord class, I had studied in church schools and had been sent abroad to study in America. Upon my return, I taught in bourgeois schools. My world outlook naturally became bourgeois and I wished to safeguard the bourgeois interests. In a meeting at our school, I delivered a speech on "the opinions of old teachers." In the speech, I exposed my bourgeois standpoint and criticized the leadership of our school. At that time, the school was administered by the Party, and my conviction that the school ought to be administered by scholars meant that I opposed the Party. In 1958, I was found to be a bourgeois rightist.

The school sent several persons to persuade me to acknowledge my mistakes. The school lowered my rank and decreased my salary, and gradually I had no choice but to admit my fault. Four years later the Party deemed that I had been remolded, but it did not restore my rank and salary.

In 1958 and 1959, China's national economy made great

strides, which the Party called the Great Leap Forward. Many of the statistics used during this campaign, however, were not accurate. From 1960 to 1962, China experienced great economic difficulty due to famine. The Soviet Union broke earlier agreements and took Soviet specialists out of China, and we called this period the "natural and man-made calamity." By the end of this period, nearly everyone was sallow and emaciated. We had a difficult time, but no one in China uttered a word of complaint.

In 1958, Margaret became the bookkeeper of a clothing factory. She got along well with the workers, and joined with six other women in forming a "sisters' organization." She was the eldest sister. In 1961, she retired after becoming ill. My mother had accompanied us to Changchun a decade earlier, but in 1961, at the age of ninety, she decided to return to her old home to live with my brother. In 1963, she fell ill. Margaret went to her, and when my mother saw my wife, she was unable to speak anymore. But she smiled at her before she died.

Driven to the countryside by the Cultural Revolution

On May 16, 1966, the Cultural Revolution began on a spectacular scale throughout the country. The revolutionaries focused the campaign against persons in power who were taking the capitalist road. (They were called capitalist roaders.) Revolutionaries paraded former government leaders through the streets, exposing them to the public. Many were imprisoned and later put to death by the Gang of Four.

The Red Guards went into the streets every day to demonstrate, shouting "It is right to rebel!" The masses were broken up politically into different factions. Each one thought that it alone was revolutionary and that all others were counterrevolutionary. The factions fought each other. During this time, the cult of individual worship of Mao Tse-tung reached its utmost height.

At our school, all work stopped. Our family was drawn into the whirlpool of the movement. Two of my wife's brothers died while doing labor at a reform camp. My daughter Alice and her husband, Guo Lin-cheng, were hospitalized for three years for wounds sustained during the Cultural Revolution. My son-in-law, although not a member of a student faction, had sympathized with one faction. One evening in 1967, the leader of the rival faction forced Alice and Lin-cheng from their home into a basement room where a student with an automatic rifle opened fire on them. Both were seriously wounded. Their four-year-old son, Guo Xu, came to live with us during their years of hospitalization and recuperation.

In the late 1950s, during the antirightist movement, I had confessed all my problems without concealing a single one. However, I had to do it again during the Cultural Revolution. Together with other old teachers, I went to school every day to write "hand-over materials" in a room guarded by soldiers. Revolutionaries searched my home and burned all my religious books, including the Bible. My second daughter worked in a factory in Inner Mongolia. She was denounced publicly by the Red Guards because of me. My sons were relatively young at the time of the Cultural Revolution, but even they did not escape its effects.

James Liu thought that I died during the Cultural Revolution. I believed that James had died. Everyone had to hand over his lifelong record of service to the leading revolutionary group, which then sent its members to find witnesses who could confirm the report. James and I were the best witnesses for each other, but no one came to see either of us for confirmation. As a result, we each thought that the other had died.

At the end of 1969, all the old teachers and administrators were sent to the countryside. Margaret and I lived there for four years. I was in charge of watching the pigs and chickens so that they wouldn't spoil the crops. Sometimes I went around the village to collect manure. In my neighborhood, several young people also were assigned to labor on the farm. In the evenings, they came to my house to listen to the radio and we became good friends.

Other members of the commune often visited me, and I discussed with them the use of fertilizer and farm chemicals. We talked occasionally of national affairs and world news. I made many friends in the countryside during those four years and gradually became a creditor in the village. When I loaned money to people, I sometimes added stipulations, for example: work harder, do not gamble, do not quarrel with your wife.

Our daily life in the countryside was relatively good. We bought grain and flour from Shuangshan, a market town three miles from our village. We also had nonstaple foodstuffs: meat, eggs, milk, and vegetables. The neighbors supplied our eggs. I fed a goat for milk. I had a nice vegetable garden in which I grew corn, beans, spinach, tomatoes, peppers, onions, cucumbers, and chives. During summer vacations and Chinese New Year's holidays, our children and grandchildren came to visit us. I became relaxed, carefree, and happy.

In 1973, I was called back to the school, and the next year I retired. In 1978, after the demise of the Gang of Four and the death of Mao Tse-tung, the new leaders of the Party announced that they would rehabilitate the rightists, of which I was one. The government restored my professional rank and salary, and returned to me all the materials listing my offenses that I had earlier submitted. I burned the materials right away. From that time on, I worked as usual in the school.

The fact that the Chinese Communist party corrected the mistakes it had committed twenty years earlier demonstrates its practical and realistic spirit. I had never thought that I could return to the revolutionary rank. My family was very happy.

Saved from poverty by mission schools

I have experienced three different power structures in China's history: the Qing Dynasty, the Guomindang Domination, and the new Socialist society following liberation. I am now more than eighty years old. I have learned many lessons that I wish to pass on to my children and grandchildren.

Altogether, we had eight children. Our three eldest died during the war of resistance against Japan, but beginning in 1940, we had two girls and then three boys. These five, Wang Ai-li, Wang Yeu-li, Wang Ji-xin, Wang You-xin, and Wang Wei-xin, are all married and have their own families. Our children have gone into the following occupations, respectively: psychology professor at Jilin University; engineer in a boiler factory; coach of hockey and speed skating; engineer in a paper factory; Olympic figure skating coach.

Their respective spouses, Guo Lin-cheng, Shi De-xiang, Nie Jing-mei, Wang Jing-fu, and Guan Yuan-rui are engaged in the following work: Changchun government official; engineer in a machine tool factory; two high school teachers; coach of figure skating. Margaret and I have nine grandchildren. Our oldest, Guo Xu, is majoring in international law at Beijing University (formerly Yenjing University), my alma mater.

Many people, including my children, have wondered how I grew up in a poor family and was able to become a professor in a university. My daughter Alice and her husband went to my native village, Wang Tun in Henan Province, and stayed for about a week to learn more about my family background. The visit confirmed for them that I had come from a poor peasant family. In 1982, when I visited the United States, I found a picture of my family at the Mennonite Library and Archives on the Bethel College campus. This picture proved further that my family background was very poor. I could not have gone to school for even one year without the help of the church. I give credit for my education—from primary school to the university to going abroad—wholly to Mennonite missions, both in China and in the United States.

Our children grew up in a different environment than ours, and therefore, they have a different world outlook. How to train them to have an outlook in accord with ours is a problem that I often think about. They were educated under the atheistic Communist government. Our children respect our Christian faith, but find it hard to accept the religious faith for themselves. It is rather hard to force my children and grandchildren to believe in Christianity, but they may sense someday that it is better to have Christian faith.

For a long time, I have had the idea of sending one of my children to America in order to become acquainted with the Christian faith. Fortunately, my grandson, Guo Xu, recently went to Nanjing to do practice teaching and obtained a Bible at Nanjing Seminary. After reading some chapters, he told me that he is very interested in Christianity and will continue to study its philosophy.

No contradiction between socialism and religion

This marvel of Chinese young people beginning to believe in Christianity illustrates that our society needs something more than science, the social sciences, and literature. People want to have a spiritual life. More seminaries like the one in Nanjing are needed. Some universities have begun to offer a course on the philosophies of the three great religions: Christianity, Buddhism, and Islam.

I have told my children and grandchildren that a person must have a conviction. There is no contradiction between socialism and religion; in present-day China, religion is legal and rightful. Everyone in China enjoys freedom of religion, which the government guarantees through the Constitution. In Changchun, I still attend church. Before liberation, the city had four Protestant churches; after liberation, they were united. I am a Christian and a state cadre at the same time. The Christian faith demands of me that I be a good state cadre.

The people of both China and the United States have a deep love for peace. Although the social systems of our two countries are different, we have many common interests. At present, the only obstacle in the development of normal diplomatic relations is the problem of Taiwan.

I have told my children and grandchildren that a person must have conviction: Margaret and Stephen with their family on Chinese New Year 1981 in Changchun.

Hand in hand, Chinese and American citizens ought to oppose nuclear war and the arms race. Both of our nations have large populations and large territory. If our nations can live in harmony from generation to generation, we will promote peace in the world.

China had a magnificent ancient civilization. Hard work and thrift have been moral strengths of the Chinese people since antiquity. Traditionally, the Chinese reinforced these values through the teachings of Confucius and Mencius, a poor boy who worked at spinning and weaving and eventually became the sage of China. Today, all Chinese consider hard work and thriftiness the key to a good life. I have instructed my children to be fair-minded, so that they might enjoy the sympathy, love, and esteem of the people. And finally, I have instructed them to ardently love labor, ardently love the motherland, and ardently love peace.

11. Letters to friends

James Liu

[During a five-year period from 1979 to 1984, James Liu wrote at least thirty-five letters to his friends in America, Wilbert Lind and Marie Regier Janzen. The early letters represent a cautious effort to renew communication. At first guarded and general, James gradually revealed his spiritual convictions, the reemergence of the church, and his views on contemporary events.

[Although for thirty years he had no opportunity to read or speak English, his facility with the language is remarkable. One notes his use of colloquialisms: How time flies; Christmas is just around the corner; Well, we'll sign off now. In each letter, he reported of Hazel's health, which declined until her death on August 16, 1984. In almost every letter, he wrote of his son Wer (later spoken of as Timothy), Timothy's wife Edna, and their two sons, Paul and John. He wrote often of the family's joy in listening to English on their newly acquired radio. He inquired about missionaries, children of missionaries, and friends of fifty years ago whom he learned to know while attending Bluffton and Bethel colleges. In later letters, he frequently quoted from Scripture.

[James Liu began writing letters to his MCC and mission friends in the West thirty months after the death of Mao and the fall of the Gang of Four. Following are excerpts of his letters to Marie Regier Janzen and Wilbert Lind.]

January 14, 1979. *Dear Miss Regier*: How time flies! It is more than thirty years since I saw you last. . . . China is changing rapidly. . . . The living standard of the people as a whole is much higher than when you were here.

May 13, 1979. *Dear Bert*: Was that a pleasant surprise to get your letter! Was I thrilled! . . . Since the day China and the States began to establish diplomatic relations, I had been thinking of writing you, but could not find your address.

May 15, 1979. *Dear Mrs. Marie Janzen*: We felt deeply sorry to hear that some of our missionary friends had passed away. We heartily sympathize with their relatives. . . .

June 25, 1979. *Dear Marie*: We have lived here in Hengyang for thirty-one years. . . . We rent a house. It has two rooms, one for our son and the other one for us. . . . We live a simple life. . . . Many people want to buy radios and phonographs through which they can study English.

June 28, 1979. *Dear Bert*: The pictures you sent us are really interesting. We had forgotten when and where they were taken. We lost ours. During the few days before liberation, the Kuomintang soldiers took all of our things away. . . . Next time you and your wife come to visit China, we will surely serve you sweet and sour fish. . . . Bert, do you still know how to use chopsticks?

August 10, 1979. *Dear Marie*: There is not a church in Hengyang, nor a house church. The only church we have here is heart-church. We have church in our hearts.

October 8, 1979. *Dear Marie*: Yes, we do need Bibles but now is not the time for us to have them, so for the time being please don't send them. It won't be long [and] I will write you for them. In general, things are turning to the good.

November 20, 1979. *Dear Bert*: Last evening, when Wer [Timothy] came home I told him right away about the books. He looked over them and said, "Now I have good English textbooks to study, and I will study hard." Bert, thank you again for these books.

January 8, 1980. *Dear Bert*: Wer went to Shanghai on December 27 and bought a Red Light radio which is the best in quality. Our grandchildren are very glad to have the radio. They can have English lessons through it every day. We can get broadcasts not only from different places in China, but programs from abroad, too. . . . We surely appreciate your help in purchasing the radio.

When Wer came back, he told us that in Shanghai the Christian churches have Sunday worship services now. How hungry the people are for spiritual food! Praise the Lord!

January 19, 1980. *Dear Marie*: You inquired about Stephen Wang. I got his last letter from Lan Chow (Lanzhou) University in 1946. I have not heard from him since then. I don't know whether he is alive or dead.

The former church leaders in Hengyang have talked about starting church work but we don't know how soon. . . . We hope the sooner the better. Let's pray for it.

March 14, 1980. *Dear Bert*: Yes, Dr. E. G. Kaufman went home on February 14. Marie J. Janzen . . . wrote about the memorial service. I could not read Marie's letter without tears. Dr. Kaufman was the first principal of our mission school. He made it possible for me to get higher education. . . . I will never forget him.

June 13, 1980. *Dear Marie*: Yes, I was very glad that I had a chance to meet Winfield [Fretz] in Shanghai, talk together, and go to church together. It was wonderful to meet him since we had not seen each other for fifty years. I still hope that I can see him again sometime in the near future. . . . We were so glad that Winfield brought us some Bibles and Christian hymns. Praise the Lord!

September 3, 1980. *Dear Bert*: Bert, I tell you good news. Bethel College, North Newton, Kansas, invited us to visit and to be guests of the college. We accepted the invitation.

October 28, 1980. *Dear Bert*: Several days ago we were informed that our government did not grant our request. . . . A verse that has been especially meaningful to us over the past few days is Romans 8:28.

January 20, 1981. *Dear Bert*: I like to think back to our days in Hengyang together when groups of children would serenade at different homes on Christmas Eve. . . . Sometimes children from the former orphanage visit us and ask, "Where is Lin Pe Pe (Uncle Lind) and what is he doing?" They have not forgotten you.

Bert, I'll tell you how I retain my hair. I don't worry much about things. I take it easy and I don't get angry easily. This is not an experiment but this is just the way I have been doing things.

August 23, 1981. *Dear Marie*: We are sorry that we don't know much about the friends and fellow Christians in Puyang (formerly Kaizhou). We have only heard that the Christians have worship services in private homes.

Yes, Stephen Wang is still living. He is teaching in Northeastern Normal University in Zhangchun, Kirin Province. . . . He was in Hengyang in May to visit us for two days.

September 4, 1981. *Dear Bert*: The text of the booklet you sent us is Mark 11:24. Hazel recited it many, many times and also asked me to memorize it. I did, too. This booklet is a great help to us in our spiritual life.

December 5, 1981. *Dear Bert*: In October, I went to Peking to meet Dr. J. Winfield Fretz, who took a group of Mennonite friends to visit China. He did not know where to find me and I did not know where he was staying. Praise the Lord that He had prepared a way for us to meet each other. There were many foreign visitors in the Summer Palace. On the third day that I went to the Summer Palace, I asked a woman, "Are you from the States?" "Yes," she said, "Are you looking for Dr. Fretz?" I said, "Yes." She said, "There he is." So we met and had a wonderful time together, but the time was too short.

July 1, 1982. *Dear Marie*: I am very glad to tell you that we have a regular church building now which is under repair. Soon we will have worship service in the church. Praise the Lord!

We received the story book *Tom Sawyer*. Paul, our elder grandson, likes it very much.

August 10, 1982. *Dear Bert*: In early June, there were two groups of Mennonite people visiting China. Among them there were quite a few former missionaries' children. I was sorry that I didn't get to meet them because I could not leave Hazel. I sent our son, Timothy, to meet one of the groups in Peking.

January 28, 1983. *Dear Marie*: On Christmas Eve, the first celebration meeting was held in the new church. The attendance was about one hundred, including a few non-Christians. Everybody was happy because we have not had a worship service in church for so long. Pastor Zhou . . . talked about the meaning of Christmas. . . . Then the Christians talked about their experiences in faith in the past years. . . . The youngest was about fifty years old. Surely we need to have young people become Christians. Let's pray for it.

June 25, 1983. *Dear Bert*: Mr. and Mrs. Hugh Sprunger came and attended the Hengyang church. We were glad to have them in our home as guests. At the Hengyang church, we have one regular pastor . . . and a church committee of nine who make plans for the church. I am one of them. Pray for the church, please.

Epilogue

In April 1980, on a trip to China, J. Winfield Fretz carried with him a letter of invitation for James and Hazel Liu. The letter from Robert Kreider, then acting dean of Bethel College, asked the couple to visit James's alma maters, Bluffton College and Bethel College. The Lius were unable to obtain passports. On February 19, 1982, President Harold J. Schultz of Bethel extended a second invitation, this time not only to James Liu but also to Stephen Wang, whose presence had become known only a few months before. Ill health and subsequently the denial of a passport prevented Liu from accepting. Wang, however, was granted a passport and came in June 1982, the fiftieth anniversary year of their graduation from Bethel College. His tour included visits to Bethel College and churches in central Kansas; Mennonite Biblical Seminary, Elkhart, Indiana; and friends in the Goshen, Indiana, community; the Bluffton College community; Mennonite Central Committee headquarters at Akron, Pennsylvania, where he met with the MCC Executive Committee; Bluffton alumni friends in eastern Pennsylvania; Washington, D.C.; Dr. C. L. and Clara Pannabecker in Pinellas Park, Florida; and Grace Liu Yang in Skokie, Illinois.

He met missionary colleagues such as Matilda Voth, Marie Regier Janzen, Elizabeth Goertz, and Dr. C. L. Pannabecker. He met the children of missionaries. At Bluffton College, he met his chemistry professor, Herbert W. Berky, then in his nineties. Many commented on Stephen's facility with English, his tireless energy and curiosity about contemporary American society, and his gift of

They envisioned a church that would be both Anabaptist and Chinese: James and son Timothy bring their message to Bethel College President Harold Schultz.

recall of names and places.

On his return to Changchun, Stephen wrote: "My visit to your country is just like a dream, but much better than a dream, because I saw my alma maters, my old friends, and alumni. I am grateful for the opportunity to renew long-standing friendships which are not only personal but reflect the strengthening of friendships between American and Chinese people. . . . I'll remember your friendliness and kindness for the rest of my life."

In 1984, Hazel Liu died after a long illness. Chinese regulations on foreign travel had been relaxed. In 1985, James Liu received a third invitation, one which also included his son Timothy. James and Timothy received passports. Their schedule included central Kansas; a meeting in Kansas City with the Commission on Overseas Mission; a China MCC reunion at Goshen, Indiana; the Bluffton College community; MCC and the Eastern Mennonite Board of Missions in Pennsylvania; Washington, D. C.; the Pannabecker family in Florida; Grace Liu Yang in Skokie, Illinois; MCC Canada and churches in Winnipeg; churches in the Vancouver area; and Mennonites in Tokyo. While James was in Florida, Timothy visited relatives of his wife's in Massachusetts.

When they returned to Hengyang, James Liu wrote many letters to his friends in North America, thanking them for happy memories. He wrote of the friendliness of people everywhere: "They provided everything we needed. We visited two Chinese Mennonite churches in Vancouver. The Christians were so nice to us. When I talked in the church in Mandarin, the pastor had to translate for me because most of them came from Guangdon Province where they speak Cantonese. Finally, I had to talk in English because some of them can only speak English."

C. L. Pannabecker wrote appreciatively of James's visit: "We met James at the airport and I was impressed how he grasped my hands and we hung together . . . there was close friendship and fellowship all through until the final fond farewell. . . . He was an ideal guest. . . . His gentle friendliness impressed all who met him and his life story of devotion and Christian love amazed all." In retrospect, the visits of Stephen Wang and James Liu were pilgrimages through North America, celebrating the fellowship of Chinese and Americans whose lives have been intertwined through decades of faithful service.

In the stories of James and Stephen are mingled both joy and sadness. Here were two talented young men, possessing love for both their church and their people. They envisioned a faith community which would be both Anabaptist and Chinese. One ponders what might have been the fulfillment of their dreams had they and their fellow believers not been engulfed by invasion, civil war, and a tidal wave of revolutionary events. And yet in their stories is evidence of victory in adversity.

The words of the Apostle Paul are appropriate to the lives of James from the village of Hua Yuan Tun and Stephen from the village of Wang:

> For I am persuaded that neither death, nor life, nor angels, nor principalities, nor powers, nor things present, nor things to come, nor height, nor depth, nor any other creature, shall be able to separate us from the love of God, which is in Christ Jesus our Lord.
> —Romans 8:38-39 (KJV)

Acknowledgments

Pivotal to the preparation of this twin autobiography has been the cheerful, prompt and diligent work of James Liu and Stephen Wang. We are grateful that they opened to us their life stories, writing skillfully in the English language, which for each had lain dormant for a generation. Rachel Waltner Goossen, in consultation with Robert Kreider, edited the manuscripts, abridging and collating the two autobiographies to provide an integrated narrative. Robert Kreider corresponded with the authors, supervised the project, and wrote the introductions to each section. The original manuscripts and correspondence with the authors from 1982 to 1987 are deposited in the Mennonite Library and Archives, North Newton, Kansas.

Winfield Fretz, Maynard Shelly, and James Juhnke served as readers. Marie Regier Frantz Janzen and the late C. Lloyd Pannabecker read portions of the autobiographies and posed questions for clarification. During a 1987 trip to China, Wilbert Lind took the completed manuscripts along for a final reading by James Liu in Hengyang and Stephen Wang in Changchun. Dr. Fretz, a college mate of James Liu and Stephen Wang, was an invaluable colleague in planning and fund raising. Rosemary Moyer made photographs available from the extensive collection of China photographs in the Mennonite Library and Archives. Thanks goes to the MLA for space and services during the course of this project.

The visits to North America of Stephen Wang in 1982 and James Liu in 1985 were essential to the completion of this project.

Major gifts by the Mennonite Central Committee, Mennonite Central Committee Canada, China Educational Exchange, Commission on Overseas Mission, Eastern Mennonite Board of Missions and Charities, and individual donors made the visits possible.

Many friends of James Liu and Stephen Wang contributed approximately three thousand dollars to cover costs of the final editing of this volume. These patrons are as follows: Elizabeth Beyler, Gladys Beyler, Stanley and Anita Bohn, Gordon and Grace Burner, Robert and Phyllis Carlson, M. A. and LaVonda Claassen, Homer and Mildred Clemens, Henry and Catherine Detwiler, Eastern Mennonite Board, Tina Ediger, John and Bernice Esau, Ruth A. Fisher, J. W. and Marguerite Fretz, Millard and Evelyn Fretz, Stanley and Gladys Fretz, Waldo H. Friesen, Walter and Harriett Gaeddert, Harry and Elva Gascho, Erwin and Verna Goering, James and Anna Juhnke, Clinton and Rosa Kaufman, Edna Kaufman, Gordon and Dorothy Kaufman, Peter and Sue Kehler, John H. Keller, Robert and Lois Kreider, Gerald and Helen Kriebel, Elvira D. Lehman, Titus Lehman, Wilbert and Rhoda Lind, Ruth Martin, Mennonite Central Committee, MCC Canada, Adam and Amelia Mueller, Elmer and La Vera Neufeld, Ida Mae Nickel, C. L. and Clara Pannabecker, Richard and Wanda Pannabecker, Willard and Ruth Peters, Robert and Alice Ruth Ramseyer, Mary Light Reed, Henry T. and Elizabeth Reimer, Erwin and Angela Rempel, Edwin J. and Vera Schrag, J. O. and Esther Schrag, Carl F. and Irene Smucker, John and Sharon Sommer, Ralph and Frances Sommer, Dallas Voran, Marie and Martha Voth, Paul and Selma Voth, Stanley E. and Elsie Voth, Waldo and Emma Voth, Orlando and Vernelle Waltner, Robert H. and Cleva Waltner, David and Martha Wedel, Malcolm and Esther Wenger, Harold and Lucinda Wik, Paul and Esther Zerger.

The advance purchase of copies of this book by the following institutions has made its publication possible: Commission on Overseas Mission of the General Conference Mennonite Church, the Eastern Board of Missions and Charities, the Mennonite Central Committee, the China Educational Exchange, Bluffton College, and Bethel College.

Finally, thanks goes to John Sommer and colleagues of the Commission on Overseas Mission for encouragement to prepare this volume, and to Faith and Life Press for accepting the responsibilities of publication.

Robert Kreider

Index

Ai Chu Tuan, 47
ancestor worship, 5, 92
Anyang, 12, 28, 74, 91

Bai Yun-xue, 53
Bartel, Henry C., 1, 2
Bartel, Nellie Schmidt, 1, 2
Beahn, Frank, x, 57, 76
Beidaiho, 46
Beijing, xi, xii, 3, 27, 29, 30, 32, 45, 46, 47, 51, 55, 57, 60, 72, 104
Beijing Normal University, 69, 72
Beijing University, 99
Berky, Herbert W., 38, 107
Bethel College, 38, 39, 40, 42, 99, 104, 107
Beyler, Clayton, xii
Beyler, Elizabeth, xii
Binying school, 12
Bluffton College, 34, 36, 37, 38, 40, 107
Boehr, Frieda Sprunger, x, 57
Boehr, Jennie Gottschall, 14, 23
Boehr, John, 36
Boehr, Peter J., x, 14, 16, 22, 50, 57; photo, 16, 17
Brown, Henry J., 1, 2, 4, 5, 16, 17, 21, 23, 49, 60, 74, 75; photo, 48, 58
Brown, Maria Miller, 1, 2, 17, 21, 60; photo, 58
Brown, Roland, xii
Brown, Sophie, xii
Burcky, Andrew C., 38
Burkholder, Lawrence, x

Canton. See Guangzhou.
Central Committee of Technical Air Defense, 71
Chang Ching, 57
Chang Shi-lu, 92
Chang Yuan, 92
Changchun, xi, 94, 95, 99, 100, 108
Changsha, 74
Chang-Yuan, 59
Cheng Guojun, 12
Chengan, 51, 52, 53, 63
Chengchou. See Zhengzhou.
Chengdu, 87
Chenggu, 69, 70
Chihli Province. See Hebei.
China Educational Exchange, xi, xii, 81, 82, 111

Chinese churches, v, xiii, 91
Chinese Foreign Relief Unit, 30
Chinese People's Liberation Army, 71
Chinese Protestant Church, 91
Chongqing, 57
Christian Fellowship, 26
Ch-Hsien-Chen, 88
Ci-xian, 63
Claassen, Lavonda, xii
Claassen, Milton, xii
Clemens, Homer, 38
Commission on Overseas Mission, xii, 111
Communist party, 14, 15, 26, 28, 32, 43, 46, 47, 54, 56, 57, 58, 59, 61, 69, 71, 72, 78, 79, 81, 83, 84, 86, 90, 91, 95, 96, 99
Cultural Revolution, vi, x, 55, 71, 74, 77, 78, 80, 81, 83, 84, 86, 88, 91, 94, 96, 97, 98

Daming, 51, 53, 55, 60, 63
Damingfu, 14, 50
Davis, Etta, 56; photo, 58
Deng Xiaoping, x, 81, 84
Dezhou, 24, 26, 27, 28, 29, 33
Dirks, Frieda Albrecht, 56; photo, 58
Dirks, Marvin, 56; photo, 58
Dirks, Marvin, Jr., photo, 58
Doell, J. H., 40
Dongming, 5

Eastern Mennonite Board of Missions and Charities, 111
economic reforms, 85
Evangelist Wang, photo, 17
Ewert, August, 15; photo, 58
Ewert, David, photo, 58
Ewert, Irene, photo, 58
Ewert, Martha Wiens, 15; photo, 58
Ewert, Philipp, photo, 58
Ewert, Ralph, photo, 58

famine, 7, 11
Fan Yong-kan, 67
farming, 6, 85
Fast, Aganetha, 22, 50, 52, 53; photo 58
Feng Yu-hsiang, 15, 16, 32; photo, 16
First High School, 76

foot-binding, 12
Fourth Hospital, 76
Fretz, J. Winfield, xi, xii, 37, 103, 104, 107
Fu Kou, 74

Gaeddert, Albert, 40
Gaeddert, Jessie Brown, xii
Gaeddert, Menno, xii
Gang of Four, 81, 84, 99
Gansu Province, xi, 70
General Conference Mennonite Mission, 7, 12, 17; map, 13
Goering, Pauline Miller, 14, 22
Goering, Samuel J., 14, 22, 33, 49, 50
Goertz, Elizabeth, 14, 15, 16, 23, 56, 57, 60; photo, 58
Goossen, Rachel Waltner, 110
Graber, Glen, 74
Great Leap Forward, x, 80, 82, 97
Guan Yuan-rui, 99
Guangdon Province, 109
Guangzhou, 50, 74, 77, 78
Guo Lan-tian, 55
Guo Lin-cheng, 99
Guo Xu, 97, 99, 100
Guomindang, 5, 32, 46, 54, 55, 58, 65, 69, 71, 72, 75, 76, 94, 95, 99

Habegger, Christine, 14
Habegger, Joseph, 35
Handan, 63
Hebei Province, 2, 3, 15, 18, 51, 66
Henan Province, 24, 25, 47, 50, 60, 61, 63, 65, 66, 67, 68, 69, 72, 73, 79, 88, 99
Henan University, 68, 93
Henan-Hebei-Shandong border region, 61
Hengyang, x, xi, 47, 57, 74, 75, 76, 77, 82, 86, 88, 91, 92, 93, 102, 103, 104, 105, 109
Hengyang Presbyterian Church, 76
Herr, Aaron, 74
Herr, Marie, 74
Hobei Province. See Hebei.
Honan Province, 2, 46, 88, 89
Hong Kong, 76, 88, 93
Hong Lo Miao, 76
Hong-zhang, 65, 66
Hopeh Province. See Hebei.
Hopei Province. See Hebei.

house church, 92, 103
Hsieh Shi-shen, 90
Hsindu, 87
Hsin-Hsiang, 60
Hu, Paul, 89
Hu Delu, 12
Hu Hsin Yu, photo, 35
Hu Lan-xiang (Edna), 82
Hua Guo-feng, 84
Hua Mei High School, 45, 49, 50, 54, 60
Hua Mei Junior High, 24, 25, 61
Hua Mei School, 18, 20, 40, 89; photo, 24, 31
Hua Yuan Tun, 3, 89
Huahsien, 47
Huang Ho River, 2, 56, 58
Hujiang University, 25
Hunan Province, 47, 74
Huttenlocher, Bill, 37

Iliff School of Theology, 41
Inner Mongolia, 30 98

Jantzen, Albert, 56; photo, 58
Jantzen, Grace, photo, 58
Jantzen, Lyman, photo, 58
Jantzen, Wilma, 56; photo, 58
Janzen, Marie Regier, x, 101. See also Regier, Marie.
Japan, 35, 45
Jiang Qing, 84
Jiangxi Province, 46, 74
Jilin Province, xi, 72
Jilin University, 99
Jixian, 12

Kai Chow. See Kaizhou and Puyang.
Kaifeng, 21, 24, 25, 33, 57, 61, 65, 68, 73, 74, 89, 93
Kaifeng Girls' High School, 69
Kaizhou, x, xii, 2, 3, 4, 5, 7, 12, 14, 15, 16, 17, 18, 21, 23, 26, 27, 33, 40, 45, 47, 50, 53, 56, 58, 59, 60, 61, 63, 65, 72, 87. See also Puyang.
Kaizhou church, photo, 44
Kaizhou mission compound, map, 19
Kansu Province, see Gansu
Kaufman, Edna Ramseyer, xii
Kaufman, Edmund George, ix, x, 14, 16, 21, 22, 25, 29, 33, 34, 35, 36, 37, 38, 39, 40, 41, 42, 53, 93, 103; photo, 20, 31

Kaufman, Hazel Dester, 14, 20, 21, 22; photo, 31
Kehler, Peter, xii
Kehler, Sue, xii
Keller, John, 37, 38
Kiangsi Province. See Jiangxi.
Kirin Province, 104. See also Jilin.
Kliewer, J. W., 20, 40, 41
Korean War, x, 77, 80, 82, 95
Kreider, Robert, xii, 107, 110
Kriebel, Gerald "Chip", 38
Ku, Theodore, 76
Ku Yin-ting, 74
Kuo Chi-jung, 73
Kuomintang. See Guomindang.
Kuyf, Wilhelmina, 43; photo, 58

Lanzhou, xi, 70, 71, 72
Lanzhou University, 70, 71, 103
Lao Tzu, ix
Lehman, Metta, 14, 23
Li Guang-ming, 23
Li Pei-yu, 74
Li Xue-ming, 49, 51
Liang Wen-hua, 59
Lin Hwei-be, 74
Lind, Rhoda, 47, 77
Lind, Wilbert, 47, 74, 75, 77, 79, 88, 101
Lin-cheng, 97
Liu, Amos, 86, 88
Liu, Edna, 87, 88; photo, 85
Liu, Hazel, 47, 49, 73, 74, 75, 78, 82, 83, 84, 87, 88, 102, 107, 108; photo, 48, 73, 85
Liu, James, v, x, 1, 3-8, 17-42, 45-49, 56, 59-63, 72-79, 82-94, 98, 101-105, 107, 108; map of journeys, 62; photo, 3, 31, 35, 41, 45, 48, 73, 85
Liu, John, xi, 82, 86, 88; photo, 85
Liu, Paul, 82, 86, 104; photo, 85
Liu, Timothy, xi, xii, 47, 61, 73, 74, 82, 87, 88, 103, 108; photo, 73, 85
Liu Chung-an (Peter), 86
Liu De-yun, 90
Liu Guo Xiang, 12
Liu Jin-O, 89
Liu Lien-hsing, 4, 7
Liu Shao-Qi, 84
Liu Tsuan-hsing, 5

Liu Wei-hsing, 4
Liu Wen-hsing, 5
Liu Yanzhou, 66, 68
Liu Yue-king, 20
Liu Yu-king, 4
Liu Zhang-fu. See Liu, James.
Liu Zhung-shan, 90
Liu Zi-qian, 69
Lohrentz, Abraham M., 14, 16, 22, 33, 39
Lohrentz, Marie Wollmann, 14, 22, 25; photo, 31
Long March, 45, 46; map, 62
Love the Lord Society, 47; photo, 45
Luo-yang, 70

Manchuria, xi, 46, 72, 94
Mao Tse-tung, ix, 45, 71, 81, 84, 97, 99
Mennonite Central Committee, x, 56, 57, 58, 72, 88, 93 94, 111
Mennonite Central Committee Canada, 111
Mennonite Library and Archives, ii, 99, 110
Mennonite mission hospital, Kaizhou, 28
Mitchell, Frank, 37
Mosiman, Leora, 37
Mosiman, Samuel K., 34, 36, 38
Mueller, A. Theodore, 40
Muzhen Girls' Senior High School, 51

Nanjing, 16, 28, 50, 57, 59, 100
Nanjing Seminary, 100
Nanjing University, 46
Nanking. See Nanjing.
Nano, 63
National First Senior High School, 65
Nebel, Dale, 94
Neufeld, Talitha, 14; photo, 16
Nie Jing-mei, 99
Northeast Technical Institute, xi
Northeastern Normal University, xi, 72, 94, 95, 104
Northeastern University, 70
Northwestern Agricultural College, 70
Northwestern Teacher's College, 69, 70

Pannabecker, Alice Ruth, xii; photo, 58
Pannabecker, Anita, xii; photo, 58
Pannabecker, Betty Jean, xii; photo, 58
Pannabecker, C. Lloyd, 15, 23, 28, 48, 59, 109; photo, 58
Pannabecker, Daniel, photo, 58
Pannabecker, Donald, photo, 58
Pannabecker, Lelia Roth, 15; photo, 58
Pannabecker, Richard, xii
Pannabecker, Sylvia Tschantz, 14, 22; photo, 58
Pannabecker, S. F., 14, 22, 26, 59, 72; photo, 58, 61
Pannabecker, Wanda, xii
Peitaiho. See Beidaiho.
Ping An Zhuang, 12
pinyin, xiii
Porter Senior High School, 24, 26, 28, 33, 40
Presbyterian Mission of Anyang, 11, 12
Pu-Pok, Mark, x
Puyang, 88, 89, 91, 104. See also Kaizhou.

Qilu University, 25, 27
Qingfeng, 63
Qi-Hsien, 74

Ramseyer, Robert, xii
Red Guards, 83, 84, 97, 98
Regier, Marie J., x, 22, 56, 57, 60; photo, 58
relief work, 93

San Yu school, 12
Schrag, Edwin, 88
Schultz, Harold J., 107, 108
Shaanxi Province, 45, 46
Shandong Province, 2, 23, 24, 25, 26, 27, 56, 57, 60, 87
Shanghai, x, xi, 14, 25, 46, 49, 50, 57, 74, 75, 76, 77, 79, 103
Shang-ji, 65
Shansi Province. See Shanxi.
Shantung Province. See Shandong.
Shanxi Province, 23
Shan-tai, 70
Shenyang, xi, 81
Shi De-xiang, 99
Shigang, 67, 68

Shuangshan, 98
Sichuan Province, 57, 70, 81, 87
Sino-Japanese War, 57, 59, 71, 74, 75, 99
Sprunger, Hugh D., v-vi, xii, 105
Sprunger, Janet, xii, 105
Sprunger, Frieda, 14, 16, 23
Stuart, Leighton, 32
Sun Yat-sen, 32
Sung Yun-ting, 89
Szechuan Province. See Sichuan.

Taiwan, 79, 93, 100
Tang-gu, 46
Tantou, 68
Tengxian, 23
Three evils, 95
Three Self Patriotic Movement, 90, 91
Tienjin, 26, 34, 46
Tientsin. See Tienjin.
Tingtau, 77
Tsu, Daniel, x
Tsuei Hsun, 47
Tung-ming station, 59

University of Chicago, 36
Unrau, Martha, 41

Voran, Dallas, x
Voth, Matilda Kliewer, 14, 22, 23, 53
Voth, William C., 14, 22, 53; photo, 17

Wang, Alice, 68, 70, 97, 99
Wang, Margaret, 47, 53, 54, 63, 95, 97, 98, 99; photo, 48, 52, 64, 101
Wang, Stephen, v, xi, 8-12, 17-42, 49-55, 63-72, 94-101, 103, 107; map of journeys, 62; photo, 9, 31, 35, 40, 48, 52, 54, 64, 101
Wang Ai-li, 99
Wang Hsien-chang, 47
Wang Hsien-deng, 20
Wang Hsiu-yun, 90
Wang Huan-zhang, 27
Wang Jian-jing, 63, 65; photo, 64
Wang Jian-wen, 63, 66; photo, 64
Wang Jing-fu, 99
Wang Jing-wen, 26
Wang Jiu-yun, 4
Wang Ji-xin, 99
Wang nee Lu, 10
Wang Tun, 8, 10, 11, 64, 99
Wang Wan-chu, 12, 72

Wang Wei-xin, 99
Wang Xin-fu, 27. See also Wang, Stephen.
Wang Yeu-li, 99
Wang You-xin, 99
Wang Zhih-an, 88
Wang Zhih-Chun, 93
warlords, 2, 14, 26
Wedel, P. J., 40
Wei Xiu-zhi, 54
Wei-hsien, 60
women, role of, 4, 10
World War II, 45
Wu Tung-tang, 89
Wuhan Seminary, 93

Xian, 72
Xian-Zhang, 65
Xiao-mei, 10
Xinyang, 66
Xinyang Normal High School, 66, 67, 69
Xin-xiang, 64
Xixiakon, 68
Xi-chuan, 69
Xuchang, 65, 66
Xuzhou, 28

Yang, Hazel T., 47. See also Liu, Hazel.
Yang Qi-zhou, 47
Yangtsun, 47
Yang-Gian-kuei, 47
Yang, Grace Liu, x, xi, 108
Ye Jin Qi Che Xiu Pei Chang factory, 82
Yellow River, 18, 30, 59, 64, 65, 70, 71, 73, 74, 93
Yenan, 46
Yenjing University, 27, 29, 30, 31, 32, 33, 36, 40, 99
Yi-chang, 66
Yoder, Harry, 38
Yoder, Louisa, 36
Yu Jen School of Nursing, 15, 47

Zhang Jing, 51, 53
Zhang River, 63
Zhang Rui-ling, 51; see also Wang, Margaret
Zhangchun, 11, 72, 94, 104. See also Changchun.
Zhejiang Province, 32
Zhengzhou, 57, 63, 64, 65, 72, 74, 88, 89
Zhen-ping, 68
Zhou Shaoyan, 66
Zhu De, 84
Zhu Hsien Zhen, 74
Zi Bien High School, 21, 24
Zingfeng, 26